SPALDING

WOMEN'S GOLF HANDBOOK

Cliff Schrock

A Division of Howard W. Sams & Co.

Published by Masters Press (a division of Howard W. Sams & Company)
2647 Waterfront Pkwy. E. Dr., Suite 300
Indianapolis, IN 46214

Published 1995
Printed in the United States of America

Library of Congress Cataloging-in-Publication Data

Schrock, Cliff. 1959-
The women's golf handbook / Cliff Schrock.
p. cm. -- (Spalding sports library)
At head of title: Spalding.
ISBN 1-57028-032-0
1. Golf for women--Handbooks, manuals, etc. I. Title.
II. Series.
GV966.S36 1995 95-3499
796.352'082--dc20 CIP

PREFACE

When I set out to organize a book for women golfers, I had one major goal among many minor ones: Make sure there was something in the book about women golfers.

As ridiculous as that may sound, I wanted to make sure I didn't repeat a problem I'd seen with many other books and videos that were labeled for the woman player. Upon further study of these books/videos, they didn't include anything specific for the woman. The contents could have applied to a male, junior, senior, anyone. I would look at the product and afterwards wonder what had there been that specifically addressed women. I'd also feel sorry for the many women who bought the book or video expecting to get a chunk of advice and discovered that they had been overlooked.

One reason that many of the golf products intended for a certain segment of the population fail to make a sharp distinction between that group and everyone else is that so much of golf applies to everyone. The swing, rules, etiquette, and other areas, by and large, are for all golfers. Everyone learns the same swing, the same way of putting, the same Rules of Golf, the same common courtesies.

In writing this book, I do believe it accomplished what I hoped it would. There is enough woman-oriented material that the book deserves its title. From history to swing problems to business golf to women's status, you will find the *Women's Golf Handbook* provides the female golfer with the kind of information and advice useful only to them. Women will learn the same swing all other golfers learn, but also read about specific problems that affect them that don't hamper other players. Plus, the portions on how to schedule a round, play business golf, how to dress, what equipment to buy, health issues, among many other topics, will give the novice woman player an all-around education on becoming a golfer.

That, ultimately, is what anyone doing work in the women's golf field hopes to achieve. Women have been slighted in being considered legitimate participants in the game. For most of golf's history, women were seen as leisure players, not worth the effort of teaching to be proficient players who participate for the game's competitive aspects. But as each year goes by, that's exactly what most women want out of the game. Sure they want to enjoy golf with friends as an escape from a busy world, but they want to play well, too, while doing it. That's why golf instructors and merchandisers are being told to pay as much attention to the woman player as possible. They are a major part of the golf population and need to be catered to.

I believe that the future of women's golf is bright. By all indications, the atmosphere in which women play is improving, albeit on the slow side in some areas. The time will come when women can feel like a full partner with other segments of the golfing population, in particular, men. I feel this way because my wife, Mary, was a golfer once and will be again and my daughter, Joelle, will I hope one day love golf as much as I do. I want both of them, as well as all other girls and women interested in golf, to develop a desire to play golf well, to enjoy it to its fullest, and carry on its traditions to future generations. I will be pleased if this book plays a small part in that mission.

Cliff Schrock
March 1995

TABLE OF CONTENTS

ACKNOWLEDGMENTS

There are many people without which this book would not be possible. Thanks to:

Photographer Todd Dunville and his models, Marlene Floyd, Malia Solquet, Diane Daugherty, Amy Lee, and the employees of the Disney Golf Shop at the Bonnett Creek Clubhouse.

The Oronoque Village Golf and Country Club in Stratford, Conn., and its professional, John Korolyshun, plus Gerri Condon, who served as a swing model.

Photographer Dean Batchelder for taking the cover photographs.

Terry Varvel, for his assistance with the photographs.

Suzanne Lincoln, for her cover design.

And to Holly Kondras at Masters Press, for her ability to send faxes, make computer changes, make phone calls and keep her sanity all at the same time while in the book-editing process.

WOMEN'S GOLF HANDBOOK

Yes, Women Are Golfers Too

What golf means to: JoAnne Carner, LPGA Hall of Fame member. "I was a carpenter's daughter, but golf changed my life. As an amateur, it took me all over. I stayed in the homes of some wonderful people. I learned good manners there. I learned how to deal with people. Golf is a character-builder. Golf's all you, nobody else."

People who don't know the history of women in golf may presume that it is all about 500 years of restrictions, male chauvinism, and women trying to attain the lofty position men have always held. Certainly discrimination is talked about quite often today, as it deserves to be. There's no argument that women golfers have had to overcome many barriers. But while it's been an uphill struggle, women have also experienced a fair amount of influence in the game's formation.

Keep in mind that the person many historians believe was the first woman to play golf wasn't born within the last 100 years. She was Mary Queen of Scots, who lived in the 1500s and was a prominent woman who gave golf some notoriety. But as a sign of things to come for women, she was silenced by being beheaded in 1587. She had been charged in a trial with having shown indifference to her husband's murder. It seems she had decided to play golf a few days after his death.

Granted, most women golfers haven't held Mary's high status, but they've been just as much a part of the game as men have been. Women have been involved as players on a social scale for many years. Illustrations from the 1800s show women dressed in large silk hats or straw boaters, stiff-collared and long-sleeved blouses, and heavy, ankle-length skirts, with shoes poorly suited to a game played on grass. Women today can be happy they don't have to wear a "Miss Higgins," an elastic garter worn around the waist of women dressed in long skirts. Before each shot, the woman lowered her garter around the knees so that a gust of wind wouldn't blow the long, flowing skirt over the ball. It actually may have served, in some sense, as a training aid, keeping women from being too active with the lower body. By the 1920s and '30s, however, the garter was gone as skirts had risen to mid-calf.

Men were the first of the two sexes to come together in groups and organize golf clubs, such as the Honourable Company of Edinburgh Golfers in 1744, the first known men's club. We can be sure that part of the motivation for getting together was male bonding. So, the white-male private club had

Women golfers have always had style, as these American women from the early 1900s show. Golf at the time was very much a social event, thus, players dressed up for the round. Today we can look back and express amazement at how outrageously players dressed for a sport that required freedom to move about. Women's long dresses were matched by men wearing ties, long-sleeved shirts and suit coats.

its start, and women and other minority groups in the 20th century are still trying to get both feet in the door.

Men's clubs made some concessions to allow women to play, but privileges were few and restrictions many. Women eventually created their own places of sanctuary. The first women's golf club was formed in St. Andrews, Scotland, in 1867. Thereafter followed many other clubs in Europe, but most of them had playing fields that weren't more substantial than a putting green. The St. Andrews Gazette stated in an 1872 article: "Its [St. Andrews women's club] remarkable success has led to the introduction and culture of golf as a female recreation in England and elsewhere. Of course, the wielding of the club assumes a mild form under the sway of the gentler sex and has never as yet extended beyond the simple stroke of the putting green." Even in the 1880s it was estimated the St. Andrews club had 500 members, but none using anything other than a putter. In the mid- to late-1880s, however, more women's clubs had formed and the players had advanced beyond the putting green.

The first British Ladies' Amateur Championship was held in 1893, with two rounds played over the nine-hole women's course at the Lytham and St. Anne's Club. It was a modest start, but that same year saw the creation of the Ladies' Golf Union, which was formed to promote the interests of the game, assist in making a uniform set of rules, set up a handicapping system, conduct the Amateur championship, and act as mediator in disputes.

When golf began to bloom in America in the late 1800s, women were right there showing a strong interest. At most clubs, though, women were not encouraged to play, basically being told "you're always welcome but never invited." Women were the clubs' second-class citizens. When the "golferines" did play, they had to endure the wrath of men who felt they tied up movement on the course. Some clubs limited the playing time given to women. At Garden City Golf Club in New York, women could play on Monday and Friday mornings only, and had to start by 11 a.m. It was unheard of at many courses to have women play on a Saturday or Sunday. At another club, women could not play on weekdays before 11:30 a.m. or after 3 p.m., nor could they play at all on Saturdays or Sundays. Even if a club did allow women to play at any time, that still didn't guarantee equality. The Great Neck Golf Club on Long Island had no policy, but men had the right of way on the course. The women there, in fact, had a committee that acted like course rangers on the fairways and saw to it that the men were able to play without problems.

To add insult to injury, husbands would discuss the advantages of keeping women off the course in the presence of their wives. Although this kind of treatment took place around the turn of the century, you can be sure that this prejudicial behavior goes on today.

But back during the early stages of golf in the U.S., there were cases of women showing influence. Women were the moving forces at clubs to get them to play golf, and women helped the sport grow. At Shinnecock Hills on eastern Long Island, women kept interest in the game alive by encouraging their husbands to play and learning the game themselves. The women there had even won the battle of having a nine-hole course built for their own use. In another case, women from Morristown, New Jersey, built their own seven-hole course in 1894, allowing men to join for a fee since the women thought they would make good caddies. And at St. Andrew's in Yonkers, New York, women had their own nine-hole course, with an initiation fee of $5 and dues of $10. Eventually, many of these separate courses were taken away by the men-governed clubs, forcing women to fight for playing time on the courses predominantly inhabited by men.

Women's competitive golf in the United States got its start in 1895, when 13 women got together to play the first U.S. Women's Amateur at the Meadow Brook Club in Hempstead, New York. The event only went 18 holes, with Mrs. Charles S. Brown, who played at Shinnecock, winning by two strokes over Nellie Sargent. It's an example of the tough situation women faced years ago that many of them weren't even referred to by their own names, and were instead listed by the husband's name. We know Nellie Sargent's first name because she was a "Miss." But underneath the labels were women with moxie and poise. When they held this first amateur, they didn't call it a ladies' championship. It was a women's championship, meaning they didn't want the image of delicate, snooty or even elderly women. They wanted to make the point that it was women playing the game, just as the opposite sex had men's championships, not gentlemen's.

It was also during those early years that the phrase "golf widow" entered into use. When good weather came in the spring, women were happy to have the man leave the house for the golf course, giving the woman domestic peace. But the husband was more than obliging, pleased to be on the course all summer, leaving the wife stranded at home. Notice the tone of this excerpt from a New York Times article in 1916 about club restrictions on women, and see how much is still applicable today:

"Saturdays, Sundays and holidays are the days when many of the clubs put a complete or partial ban upon the fair sex in relation to the fair green. They may come to watch but not remain to play, to paraphrase the old adage. The reason behind this prohibition is not far to seek. These are the days on which the tired business man feels it—and not unjustly—his peculiar prerogative to rest and recreate. Obviously, if he is a golf player and therefore lost to other forms of outdoor sport, he wants the links to himself and his male friends, at least for a part of the day. The result is a host of varied limitations upon woman's freedom of the links."

The plight of the all-suffering wife hasn't completely left us to this day, and the golf widows of this world still fight a hard battle against isolation. But their cause has been joined by the vast number of women who have picked up the game, and who have become partners with their husbands on the course or have made their own circle of golfing friends. Probably the strongest area of influence women have had is the family country club atmosphere today, with clubs providing a variety of services in large-sized clubhouses. Clubs are much more than a place to hang your coat and hat, change shoes and have a drink, and women have helped develop that.

From that start of just 13 players in the first U.S. Women's Amateur—and some not-so-good golf—the interest in competition among women grew and great amateur players emerged, such as Margaret and Harriot Curtis, Alexa Stirling, Glenna Collett Vare and Virginia Van Wie in the United States. Joyce Wethered was Britain's preeminent amateur at the time. In 1932, the Curtis sisters, who had been enthralled by previous competitions between U.S. and British players, saw their hopes for a regular match fulfilled when the trophy they donated for such an event was used in the first Curtis Cup. This competition was helpful in encouraging women to strive for proficiency as players.

The men's professional tour had its roots in the 1920s and '30s. At this time the best women players were amateurs. But in the late 1930s and into the '40s, the finest women golfers were beginning to think about forming a women's pro tour. Golfers such as Babe Zaharias, Patty Berg, Betty Jameson, Louise Suggs, Betsy Rawls and Marilynn Smith formed the nucleus of a women's tour. The circuit had some false starts in the '40s, but the present Ladies Professional Golf Association was chartered in 1950. The tour didn't provide much of a

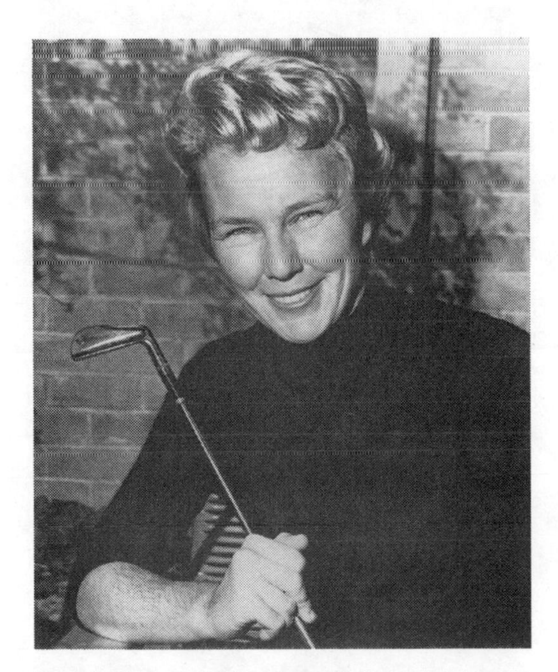

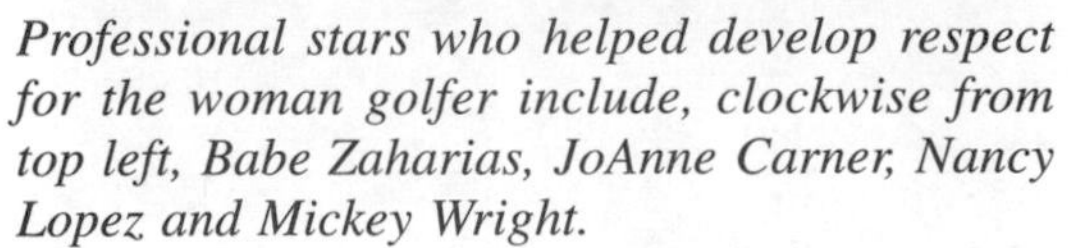

Professional stars who helped develop respect for the woman golfer include, clockwise from top left, Babe Zaharias, JoAnne Carner, Nancy Lopez and Mickey Wright.

living then, so it was the golfers who really loved the game that made the tour work. Their popularity, particularly of the legendary Zaharias, slowly established the tour on solid footing.

Mickey Wright, often given credit as having the finest swing of all time, either male or female, continued the tour's growth with her incredible play in the 1960s. In the '70s, the LPGA was holding its own when its first commissioner, Ray Volpe, was hired in 1975. Along with his creative leadership, and the popularity of new star Nancy Lopez, who debuted in 1977, the LPGA saw corporate involvement increase, tournament purses escalate, and television coverage improve. In addition to Lopez, JoAnne Carner, Pat Bradley, Patty Sheehan, Amy Alcott, Betsy King and Beth Daniel brought the tour into the 1990s with a high level of playing ability. There are now more talented players on tour than ever before. And with the steadying guidance of Charles Mechem as commissioner, the tour reversed its floundering path of the late '80s. The LPGA still ranks far behind the PGA Tour in total prize money ($25 million in 38 LPGA events for 1995 compared with the PGA's more than $55 million), but it's situated on firm ground.

It may be impossible to expect that women will ever "catch up" with men. But the health of the LPGA Tour alone is enough to show that since the game began women have aimed to be equals and have earned respect and admiration for their accomplishments. The spirit of a golfer includes determination, desire, love of the outdoors and companionship, and improving the body's physical and mental strength, among many things. There can be no arguing that women embody these traits as well as men do.

What is Golf, Anyway?

What golf means to: Judy Rankin, TV-golf announcer and former LPGA star. "Golf is responsible for every turn my life has taken, from childhood on. It established a good relationship with my father. It taught me certain kinds of discipline. I met my husband through golf and it's enriched my son's life."

There is potentially a long list of reasons why you're wanting to learn golf. Maybe it's been a goal of yours for years. Perhaps you're doing it for business reasons, to take advantage of the opportunities golf presents within the corporate world. Your intent might be to join a spouse, family or friends in a challenging activity that will provide pleasure for decades. It could be that you've been a member at a private club for many years and are switching over from tennis. It could be a bit of all of these.

There's really no limit to what brought you to the game. Its appeal is universal. It's loved by young and old, male and female. In recent years, thank goodness, we have seen a gradual easing of access barriers to minority groups. And those people inhibited by golf's financial hardships can find equipment bargains and inexpensive green fees if they look for them.

Golf has had to overcome some problems that haven't hampered popular sports such as basketball, baseball and football. Want to shoot a few hoops? Just buy a basketball and go to the local playground and shoot away. Getting onto the golf course isn't so easy, however. Things have to be done in stages. First is buying the equipment. Second is learning to swing. Third is understanding rules and etiquette. And fourth, perhaps the most difficult of all, is getting into a group on the first tee at your local course. Many areas in the United States have course shortages; not a lack of private clubs, mind you, but public-access courses. In these locations, courses are so busy that you must call for a reservation, and if you don't have one, you'll wait up to two, three or more hours for your group to set foot on the tee. Once on the course, it may take six hours to play 18 holes. This inordinate amount of playing time is one of golf's problems.

The potential headache of getting onto the course will be explained in Chapter 4. For now, let's focus on another part of the game that you'd do well to learn before playing, and that is golf's history and other background facts.

Golf isn't a recently developed sport. It goes back in time several centuries, which explains why golf is a tradition-rich game that teaches the player honesty, integrity and sportsmanship. If the player lacks in any of these areas, then he or she hasn't completely immersed themselves in the game and won't get complete satisfaction from it.

Golf wasn't developed in a day, a week or a year. It evolved for many decades before taking its current form. It had an obscure beginning, and not much is known for certain about it. Historians believe that a game that had the general concept of golf—hitting a ball or object across an open field toward a target—had its start in the 1300s. Over the years, guidelines were added that shaped the game into the present form of golf. Early players probably used one club, but agreed to add more clubs since shots were of different lengths. The target may have been a goal above ground level, but gradually became a hole in the turf. There also wasn't any opposition or defense against the player from reaching the target. The only obstacles were found in nature itself, such as the wind, trees, tall grass, streams, sandy depressions and the like. This idea that the game would not have offensive and defensive players has made it unique in the sports world.

Where did all of this begin? There have been numerous sites referred to as the birthplace of golf, such as Holland, France and China, but Scotland in the late 1300s is the accepted location and time for golf's origin. One of the first-known mentions of golf occurred in 1457 when it was banned in Scotland by King James II in the interest of military discipline. The first reference to golf in England was in the 1600s.

In Scotland, the game was spelled with an "e" at the end, golfe. The sport was played on an open field, with all the rough edges you would expect from that kind of setting. The golf course we play today in America, with its closely mown fairways and greens, is a far cry from what the first golfers played on. Their "course" was the good earth, as barren and as natural as the terrain could be.

Thousands of golfers travel each year to Scotland, as well as England and Ireland, to see where golf was first played. They lug their clubs with them because they want to play golf in as natural a setting as possible, knowing the courses there still retain a lot of the terrain's rawness and don't receive much, if any, architectural doctoring.

As you learned in Chapter 1, the private club started in the 1700s, a few centuries after the game did. In those same countries where golf began, groups of golfers came together to form clubs and play at their own courses. After the Honourable Company of Edinburgh Golfers in 1744, another club was the Royal and Ancient Golf Club of St. Andrews in 1754. Both clubs are still around today, still command a lot of respect and power, and still haven't fully embraced the idea that women can be part of a club, too.

These groups of players flourished, courses continued to be built, playing ability improved and clubs held competitive events at their courses. The world's oldest championship of major importance, the British Open for men, was begun in 1860.

The first golf club in North America was formed in 1873, the Royal Montreal Golf Club in Canada. There is evidence that golf first came to the United States in the late 1700s. This is based on references to the formation of a golf club in South Carolina in 1786. Plus, it is believed that Scottish and European settlers establishing homes in America around this time would have brought golf with them. There were probably small pockets of golfers around the colonies. Golf's real presence in the U.S., however, didn't take place until the late 1800s. That's the time when many golf clubs, like those formed in Scotland, were organized. There is great dispute about which club was the first club in the U.S., but possibly the first permanent club was the St. Andrew's Golf Club in Yonkers, New York, begun in 1888.

In the development of women's golf from infancy to maturity, character and sportsmanship have been important elements. Glenna Collett Vare (upper right) set a level of amateur excellence that still impresses today. Patty Berg (upper left, with cap) and Mickey Wright were pioneers in the formation of the LPGA Tour. Their style, grace, expert play and sportsmanship are carried on today by players such as Betsy King (right), whose charity work reflects her personal faith.

Women have been trying to catch up to the pubicity given men golfers ever since golf came to the U.S. Clubs for men only (below) were common and they intentionally limited or shut out women. Some familiar male faces include (above), from left, Byron Nelson, Dwight Eisenhower, Ben Hogan and Clifford Roberts, the latter influential in creating the Masters Tournament.

The formation of the U.S. Golf Association, the primary governing body of golf in the U.S., in 1894 helped spread golf around the country. The USGA held the first U.S. Amateur and first U.S. Open for men in 1895. From then on, competition in the United States began to flourish. The first National Collegiate Athletic Association Championship was held in 1897.

Because of the cost involved in building a golf course and clubhouse, in addition to the elitist nature of the private golf club, golf got off on the wrong foot in the U.S. It was a sport for the wealthy who socialized with each other at country clubs. That stigma has been hard to erase. When people think of golf, many of them think of a sport for the well-to-do. One need only look at the overflowing parking lot of the local public course on weekend mornings, however, to see that the game has a following, too, among those people not in a position to spend large amounts of money on it. Golf is no longer limited by the division of social classes.

Around the turn of the century, golf club professionals came over from Scotland and England to the U.S. to be a part of this new market of golf courses and players. These professionals, with a wealth of golf knowledge compared to Americans, helped lay out courses, design and make golf clubs, and teach the swing. In America they found many willing students.

Once Americans became proficient at the game and how to do the things foreigners had been doing with such proficiency, they tried to give golf their own touch. In 1916, the Professional Golfers' Association of America (PGA of America) was formed to bring course professionals together. Located on site at the golf course, these people promoted the game with great zeal. The result was a country that fell in love with the game. Some of the things Americans did to the sport, though, haven't pleased everyone. Americans added things such as electric/gas carts that purists everywhere find repulsive. But these American adaptions have a foothold in the game and aren't likely to go away.

During this century, golf has exploded into a game played by millions of people in the United States. What brought golf to where it is today in this country? There are certain events that occurred that are accepted as milestones in the development of American golf. They include:

- American amateur Francis Ouimet winning the 1913 U.S. Open against two of British golf's best players. His victory boosted American confidence that they could play the game on a level with golfers from golf's homeland.

- Bobby Jones winning the four major tournaments for men in 1930—a Grand Slam—and giving the game added exposure and prestige because of his sportsmanship and good character.

- Jones starting the first Masters Tournament in 1934.

- The PGA Tour becoming a full-fledged organization in the '30s, keeping track of its tournament schedule, players, results and money winners. The tour was a prominent vehicle for golf, putting it in a glamorous setting and showcasing how well golf can be played.

- The women's game moving into prominence following World War II. The first U.S. Women's Open was held in 1946. The Ladies Professional Golf Association (LPGA) tour was formed in 1950, and the first LPGA Championship was played in 1955. As women saw the enjoyment they could have playing golf, the industry boomed as another segment of the market opened up. (The start of the men's senior professional tour in 1980 had a similar effect on the over-age-50 segment.)

- President Eisenhower's affinity for golf while in the White House boosting its appeal, but not among the common man.
- The combination of popular star Arnold Palmer and the exposure of golf on television making golf an appealing sport to people of all ages and economic divisions.
- The effect of the three major professional U.S. tours—men, women, and senior men—on the public's fascination with golf has been enormous, from the equipment players use to the speed at which they play.
- Golf has now gone on a global boom, as the playing level of professional players worldwide has shown that it's not only Americans who can play well. Indicative of the professional players who captured people's attention, not just as players but as people who had and have something important to say about being champions are Tommy Armour, Seve Ballesteros, JoAnne Carner, Nick Faldo, Ben Hogan, Betsy King, Nancy Lopez, Byron Nelson, Jack Nicklaus, Arnold Palmer, Gene Sarazen, Sam Snead, Peter Thomson, Tom Watson and Mickey Wright.

That is a very short look at how golf got to where it is today. What is golf, anyway? You're about to find out more details as you learn about equipment, playing rules, how to set up a game, and how to swing the club. Golf is a sport that hasn't and probably won't catch up to the amount of public attention given to baseball, football and basketball. But as a sport played by 25 million people, golf is solidly planted as one of our most-popular pastimes. It's arguably the most challenging game ever created. And it clearly gives the player immense pleasure, excitement and satisfaction. Golf remains a unique sport that every day captures the fancy of numerous new players.

3 How Equipment Functions

What golf means to: Dolores Hope, wife of entertainer Bob Hope. "Bob and I could not have stood each other for so long if it had not been for golf. On our first date, we drew golf holes on the tablecloth. And playing golf helped me land Bob as a husband. It gave us something in common."

Before you set foot on the golf course, there are three areas you need to become familiar with: the course itself, the swing and how to play, and last but not least, how equipment works.

Golf equipment is more complicated than that of any other sport. There's just a ball to worry about in basketball and football. You've got a bat, ball and glove in baseball and softball. In hockey there's a puck and stick. Golfers not only have a supply of balls, but a bag, tees and up to 14 clubs. When you are set up with clubs that fit your size and playing ability, you can be confident you're ready to battle the course.

The golf club consists of a long, thin shaft with a grip made of rubber or leather at one end and a clubhead at the other. Each clubhead has a heel (which connects with the shaft), clubface (which strikes the ball), toe (rounded edge at the other end from the heel), and sole (bottom of the clubhead). And each club you carry has a different shaft length, different clubhead, and is used to perform different functions. The longest-shafted clubs, called woods, send the ball the longest distances. However, as irons get shorter, and the numbers on the clubs go up, the ball travels shorter distances.

For many centuries, golfers used clubs that had shafts made from hazel or ash wood. Hickory was later imported from America and was the standard shaft material until steel took over in the early 1900s. Steel is still the common shaft today, but newer, high-tech materials such as graphite and titanium are also popular because of their light weight and strength.

The first clubheads were also made entirely of wood. Some clubs had iron heads, but were only used to get the ball out of a depression. When steel shafts became popular, they were matched up with iron heads and became the standard club. Clubmakers eventually settled on a set of clubs that had three to four long, steel-shafted clubs with wood heads (the woods) to hit the ball a long way, and the rest of the set had steel-shafted clubs with steel heads (the irons). The standard set of clubs today includes three or four woods (which can have a wooden or metal head), and around 10 irons.

Equipment has come a long way since these early clubs and balls were the standard.

Your clubs work best when you know how far the ball goes with each one. If you need to make a shot of 160 yards and you know you can hit your 3-iron that distance, as long as there aren't any other variables to affect the shot, you'll play that club. To find out how far you hit each club, use your 5-iron distance. Hit your 5-iron, and if it goes 140 yards, then you can compute in 10-yard increments to determine the lengths you hit other clubs. Your 6-iron would travel 130 yards, 4-iron 150 and so on. Base your initial calculations on this data, then adjust as needed when you see actual distances.

Compare yourself to these average distance figures for women: Driver (190 yards), 2-wood (180), 3-wood (170), 4-wood (160), 5-wood (150), 1-iron (160), 2-iron (150), 3-iron (140), 4-iron (130), 5-iron (120), 6-iron (110), 7-iron (100), 8-iron (90), 9-iron (80), pitching wedge (70) and sand wedge (50).

Clubs hit the ball different distances because of two things. First is the length of the shaft; as noted already, longer-shafted clubs send the ball longer distances. Second is the loft of the clubface. Loft is the amount in degrees that the clubface is tilted back from being straight up and down. If you look at a 3-iron compared to a 9-iron, you see that the 3-iron has less loft. It sends the ball on a lower flight than the 9-iron, allowing the ball to fly much farther and roll a longer distance.

A third change from one club to the next is "lie." The lie of the club is the angle formed by the ground and the clubshaft. The lie becomes more upright as you go from longer-shafted clubs to shorter.

The ball was also made out of wood at one time, but it too went through a transformation. The first change was called the "feathery", a ball with a leather cover, stuffed tight with a tophat-full of feathers and sewn shut. Then ballmakers went to the gutta-percha ball around 1850. The gutta had a much firmer shell than the feathery, and was made from hardened gum. It was the hard-shell predecessor to the present ball. The gutta had a more consistent flight than the feathery and was more durable, but it also caused damage to the clubface. The gutta was eventually abandoned in the early 1900s when the rubber-cored ball, with a softer, dimpled cover, was first developed. It is that model that has been refined and reworked throughout the century to arrive at today's assortment of balls.

Getting down to basics

That gives you a ground-floor look at how manufacturers arrived at today's clubs and balls. Now let's take a look at some specifics regarding each type of club, beginning with woods.

The woods have the least loft of any club besides the putter. They are numbered from 1 (also known as the driver) to as high as 9. The most-common woods people carry are the 1, 3, 4 and 5. The 1-wood has the lowest loft, ranging from 8 to 11 degrees. The 9-wood has loft of about 20 degrees. If you're a beginner, be sure to use a driver with a higher degree of loft to get the ball airborne. The driver will send the ball the longest distance, although that may not be the case immediately if you're a new player.

The great thing about woods is not only do they hit the ball a long way, but they are user-friendly. Metal woods, for instance, have weight distributed evenly around the clubface so if the ball is mis-hit, shots aren't affected as severely. Also, if you have trouble hitting your irons, you can use the wood equivalent and usually have more success getting the ball in the air. Woods and irons with similar lofts include the following pairs: a 3-wood and the 1-iron, 4-wood and 2-iron, 5-wood and 3-iron, 7-wood and 4-iron, and 9-wood and 5-iron.

Irons are numbered from 1 to 9, plus the wedges. The lofts range from around 19 degrees for a 1-iron to 45 degrees for a 9-iron. The types of irons you see at a golf shop may look like they vary widely, but they come down to two methods of construction.

First is the forged blade, the traditional construction. Sometimes hand made, but often stamped out of machines, the forged iron is known for being the club of choice by better players. The sweet spot—the area in the middle of the clubface that has the best response on the ball at impact—is unforgiving. If you hit the ball on the perimeter of the forged clubface, ball distance is drastically shortened. Expert players like forged clubs, however, because they get good feedback on how well they hit the ball, and forged irons make the ball fly with different curvatures more easily.

The second type of iron is the cavity back club, which came along in the late 1960s and is the most popular iron today. It is an investment-cast iron, meaning it's made out of a mold. This club has the opposite affect for poor shots than the forged club. Like a metal wood, the cavity back iron has more clubhead weight distributed around the clubface. If a ball is hit off-center on this club, there is more weight behind it, and the ball still carries well and doesn't go as far off line. Because of this benefit, cavity back clubs are very popular with beginners and average players.

The shortest full-swing clubs in your set are the wedges. They have the highest loft of any club and are intended to get your ball as close to the hole as possible. Pitching wedges have lofts in the low 50s and should be used when the ball is on grass because of its wide sole. The more loft there is on the wedge, the shorter the ball will go, but the higher it will fly. That's why the lob wedge, with 60 degrees of loft, is ideal for shots under 50 yards over bunkers and small trees. The ball will fly high and land softly.

The sand wedge has loft in the mid-50s and has an even wider sole than the pitching wedge. It's a great club not only out of the sand but also from tall grass. The sand wedge has "bounce," meaning the back edge of the sole is lower than the leading edge and allows the club to deflect off the sand rather than dig into it.

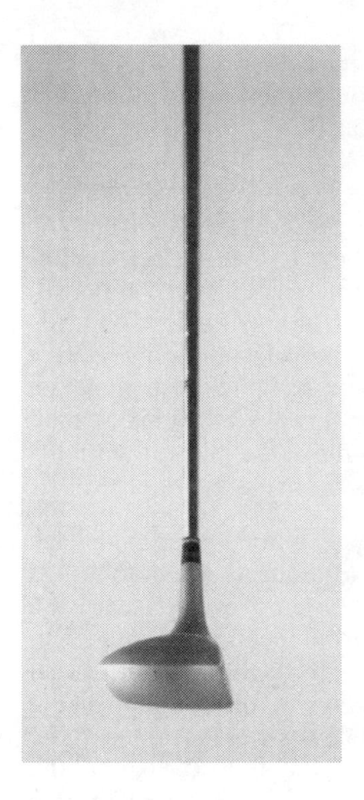

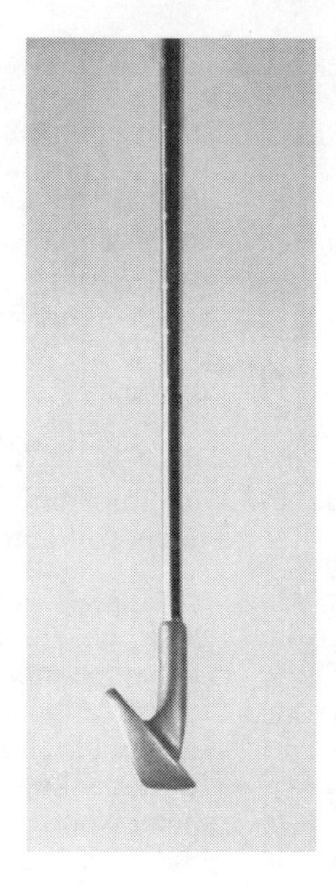

These pictures of a wood and iron show the difference in their usefulness. The wood has a less-lofted clubface and bigger head. The ball flies lower than with an iron and thus travels farther. The iron, with more loft, is usually used from the fairway as the golfer plays shots to the putting green.

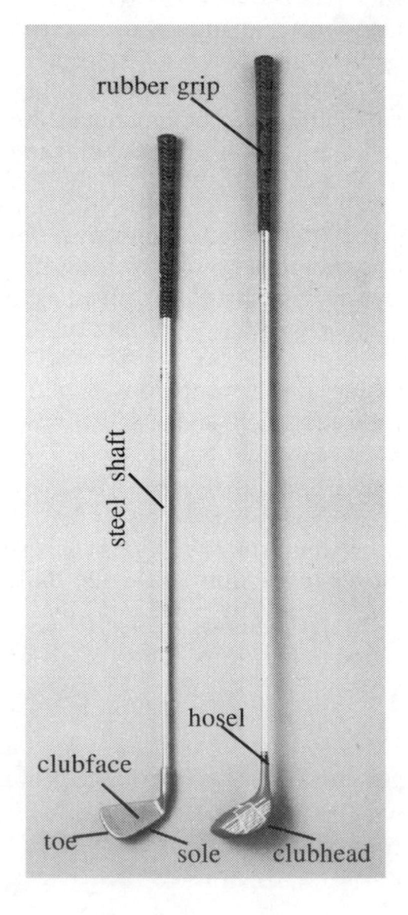

This full view of an iron and wood shows the parts of a club. Beginning from the top is a rubber grip, then the steel shaft and the clubhead itself. The hosel is the part that attaches the clubhead to the shaft. The clubface is etched with grooves. The toe of the club is opposite the hosel, and the sole is the bottom edge.

We've barely mentioned the putter, but you probably won't use a club any more often than the "flat stick," as it is called. Think of it this way. You will probably take at least two putts per hole. For 18 holes that means 36 strokes. New players will take, perhaps, three putts per hole. Now we're up to 54 putts, which is approaching the halfway mark for number of shots played by beginners.

Putters come in as many different shapes and designs as there are course designs. The best advice in picking a putter is getting one that feels the most comfortable and combine it with a proper arms-and-shoulders putting stroke. And make sure the putter has some kind of hash mark on the top of the clubhead to help with alignment and direction.

Putters are designed to give you more feel than any other club. You may find a putter you like and use it for the rest of your life. There are several shapes to choose from: the mallet (with a head that looks like a flat version of a metal driver), the blade (a thin head that connects with the shaft near its middle on top), the flange (which looks like a blade but has an extension coming out from the back of the sole), and the heel-toe weighted club (that has a cavity back like an iron and an offset hosel).

Be cautious at first

Anyone who has been around the game for a long time could testify that women's equipment has improved. It used to be that you could tell a women's set from across the room just by seeing its pink grips. Upon closer inspection you'd see daisies on the back of the clubhead and other pastel colors. Women's golf bags came in pinks and yellows, with animal motifs as decorations. The entire line of women's equipment had "dainty" written all over it.

The equipment did little to help women play. Manufacturers had done scant research on women's needs, and they hadn't put much money into producing useful, effective clubs. They didn't seem concerned that the colorful effects didn't influence the way the ball responded or the way the woman swung.

Things are moving full swing the other way, however. Women's apparel has always had the attention of designers. Now so do women's clubs. Pastels are out where equipment is concerned. Lightweight shafts, plus oversized clubheads and balls, have come along at the right time to be a part of the burgeoning women's market. Club companies test and evaluate what helps women play their best. At last the woman golfer is being taken seriously as a player, and both the club companies and golf course professionals are seeing how well women respond to quality services and goods. Club pros are trying new displays and new directions in their women's lines to see what patterns work best for buyer loyalty and repeat business.

If you're a beginner, and you've chosen to set aside your life's savings to get into the game, you have to resist the strong urge to go out and buy the most expensive set of clubs. It's been done countless times before and will continue. Unfortunately, people think if they have the priciest equipment, they'll make a swing of equal value.

Don't overestimate the importance of your clubs to your final score. It's the combination of a sound swing with quality equipment that causes excellent results. Be smart and don't fall into the trap of trying to "buy" a golf game. Think in terms of buying moderately, at first, to have clubs to learn the game. Don't put down your major money until you've reached a point with your playing ability that Grade A equipment is useful. It doesn't make sense to invest in a Steinway if you haven't learned to play "Chopsticks" yet.

Since new players usually hit most of their clubs the same length, they don't have many decisions to make when it comes to club selection. That means the fewer the clubs the better. You should buy equipment

Different ball constructions include, from left, a two-piece ball and two types of three-piece balls with an inner core and rubber winding.

that corresponds with your present talent level, then upgrade when you make significant improvement. Your first set should have one wood with loft, such as a 3-, 4- or 5-wood, plus four irons, the 3-, 5-, 7- and 9-irons, and a putter. Having a pitching wedge with 52 degrees of loft would be fine. A sand wedge of around 56 degrees could be added after playing with the first set of clubs for a while. Don't add a lob wedge with 60 degrees of loft until you've really mastered the swing.

That gives you a set of eight clubs. Since the Rules of Golf allow you 14, you have plenty of room to add more clubs after becoming proficient and having learned how to handle different weather and course situations. You have the option of getting a full set of clubs to begin with and just using the clubs mentioned above to start, or buying a beginner's set, which would have a limited number of clubs. When you're ready to add more clubs, it's best to fill in with the shorter clubs first—adding an 8-iron and so on. When you have a full set of irons, then add more woods until only the driver is needed as the final addition. You may be tempted to hit the driver first, but it's so difficult to master at the beginning that you'll enjoy the game more and be less frustrated by waiting to use it until the end. And as for the 1- and 2-irons, they are generally used by only the better players. Add them to your set only when you can hit them well and have discovered they fill a void in your playing arsenal.

Here's what you can expect to get for your money when purchasing clubs.

In the low-price range, perhaps $200 to $300, clubs are often aluminum-headed woods and zinc-headed, die-cast irons with steel shafts. The clubs aren't the best looking or feeling, but they are fine to learn with. Use these clubs to start, and you'll have good incentive to work toward the next level. You could even get away with spending less for starter clubs, perhaps finding some used clubs in the golf shop.

Clubs in the middle range, $300 to $500, feel better and therefore provide added confidence. The woods and irons are usually stainless steel with steel shafts. You could go ahead and buy a full set at this price, and only use the clubs you feel comfortable with to start and add others later.

For clubs on the high end, $500 and up, the sky's the limit. At this point, you're ready to move into something permanent and long-

When a golfer is fit for a set of clubs, he or she can expect to have a number of measurements and tests done by the clubfitter. Among them include, right, being measured from the ground up to the hand, and seeing a bag full of irons with different lofts, lies and shafts. The clubfitter uses the clubs to see which type is compatible with the player's swing and ability.

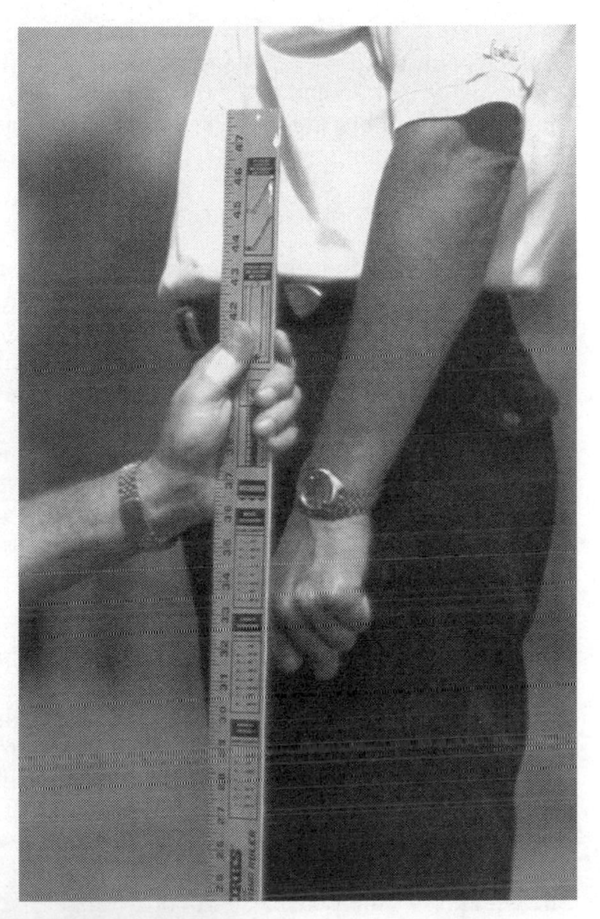

lasting. You should spend this much when you're around a 20- to 25-handicapper. Be your most selective and insist on trying out the clubs before buying. If you're ready for this purchase, your game must be fairly consistent and you must be primed to see what you can do with top-notch clubs.

Some club sellers help you buy clubs off the rack and tailor them to your size and swing shape. Others take club components—separate pieces of clubheads, shafts, grips—and piece a set together after taking measurements, such as your height and hand size, and watching you hit balls on the range. Such custom-club fitters are trained to make a set as closely in sync with your body and talent as possible. But remember, custom services, as well as special materials such as graphite and titanium, will greatly increase your cost.

Ask the professional at your course or club if they can help you with a custom-club set. If they can't, ask them to suggest someone. Or ask fellow golfing friends if they can recommend someone. If you're going to invest a lot of money in a custom set, make sure you're being fitted by someone who knows their business. There are also a number of club professionals associated with equipment companies that have custom lines or programs to create the ideal set for you.

Sorting out the variety of balls

New players will discover that the kind of ball they use won't matter a great deal compared to the type of clubs they have. Once you are a consistent ball-striker, you can experiment with the different types of performance balls to see which ones feel best. Until then, you only need a ball that will survive all the nasty blows you'll apply to it—hitting it thin, knocking it into trees and bouncing it off concrete.

Of the two primary ball types, the beginning player would benefit from using a two-piece distance ball. This ball is constructed with a hard inner core and durable outer shell, usually Surlyn. It's ideal for players who don't always hit the ball squarely, but it provides extra distance so it assists the player who doesn't hit the ball far.

The three-piece ball, built of an inner core with a rubber winding and soft outer shell called balata, is usually played by better golfers because it feels softer and can be spun easier for different types of shots. It also has a softer feel when putting, an important piece of feedback for many players. High-handicap players would be better off not playing this ball until they hit fewer bad shots. Poor hits will damage a three-piece ball, which is a costly knock to the pocketbook.

While those two balls are the ones commonly used by most golfers, manufacturers have gone even further in creating balls that can fly lower or higher, give added distance and spin more or spin less. When you have reached a good ability level, you can experiment with these balls to see whether they help you with course conditions such as wind, dry or wet ground, your own style of play, or the type of equipment you use. The idea is to match the ball with your area of need. If you hit a high ball, but need to hit lower shots on a particular course, switch to a low-trajectory ball.

Research into the women's swing has resulted in balls that are designed for a woman's slower swing speed. In the past, women used balls intended for men that had less compression. Now after studying women's swing dynamics, companies have made balls, such as Spalding's Top Flite XL-W in its women's ball series, with a soft cover and core to release the maximum amount of energy at impact from a woman's 70-mile-per-hour swing speed.

Only settle for the best

There's nothing worse than investing a substantial amount of money on something you had to rely on someone else's advice to buy, and then finding out you'd been misled. If that happens with your purchase of new clubs, you can, of course, take it back to the seller and ask for compensation. But you can save yourself that problem by reading as much as you can about equipment and making sure the shop personnel answer all your questions. For instance:

- Be sure they're not trying to sell you a set of men's clubs, unless you're a good enough player to handle them.
- Make sure your clubs have the proper size grips for your hands.
- Ask about clubs with a progressive offset since they help get the ball airborne by putting your hands ahead of the ball at address.
- Look into steel-shafted clubs with a low flex point to also make it easier to get the ball up.
- Notice how low-torque shafts help make the ball go straighter, but they may also decrease your feel. Since a woman needs torque for timing the shot, experiment with clubs with this shaft.
- Some of the advantages to big-headed drivers and irons may help you. They have larger clubfaces, perhaps 20 percent bigger, so off-center hits aren't as wildly off target.
- Test whether the oversized balls are beneficial for you. A regular ball is 1.68 inches in diameter. Oversized balls are around 1.72 inches. That doesn't seem like a major difference, but bigger balls are said to be longer and straighter for the average player.
- Ask about clubs that have aerodynamically designed clubheads that cut wind resistance and therefore increase clubhead speed. Similarly, boron and graphite shafts are lighter than steel. If put into a driver that's one inch longer than standard, it can keep the club the same weight as a shorter one but increase distance.
- Irons with a thicker head mass are designed to have a lower and deeper center of gravity, and thus provide better distance.
- Clubs with a low center of gravity get more weight under the ball, thereby getting shots up faster and higher and with more backspin.
- Check into equipment companies that not only have a standard women's length club, but also petite lengths for women who are under 5-feet 2-inches.

These are all indications of the work manufacturers are doing in the women's

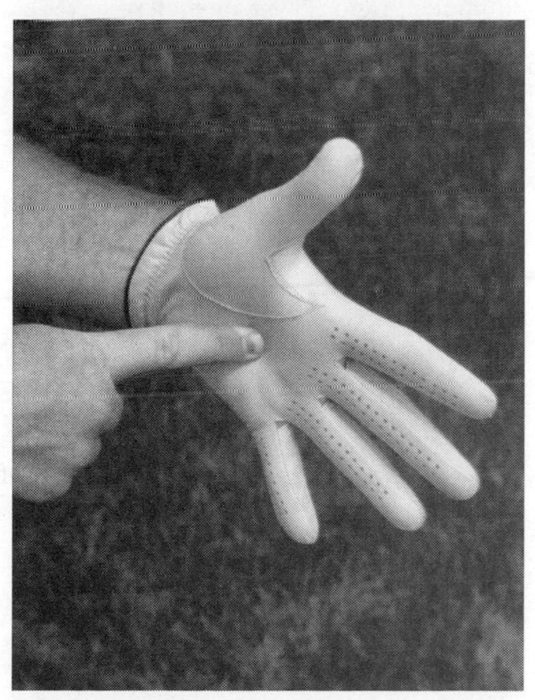

A properly fitted glove should react like the top of a drum when the palm is pressed and the fingers extended.

Within the last few years, the pop-up stand bag has become very popular. It makes it easier to pull out a club, plus saves the golfer wear and tear on his or her back.

equipment field. There are a lot of new designs that work with a woman's swing speed and method of swinging. Many of these terms and phrases might sound foreign and unintelligible to you, but by working with a qualified clubfitter or club seller, you'll be able to take advantage of these new lines. The seller should know what these features mean. If he or she doesn't, find someone who works for you to get the best set possible.

Packing your bag

Your golf bag should include more than just balls, tees and clubs. The bag itself, if you're a walker, should be one of the newer lightweight carry bags with a pop-up stand and strap that eases the weight load on your back. Be sure to get head covers to protect the woods.

The newer bags have a surprising amount of storage. Some of the things to include are a dozen balls, tees, coins for ball markers, a divot tool to fix ball marks, rain jacket or suit, a couple of cabretta-leather or synthetic-leather gloves for your left hand (for a right-hander) if you use them, a large towel to keep clubs and hands clean, sunscreen, Band-Aids, insect repellant, hat, umbrella, a Rules of Golf book, and a snack if desired.

4 GOLF'S PROCEDURES, RULES AND ETIQUETTE

What golf means to: Marilynn Smith, LPGA Hall of Fame member. "I've learned a lot from the people I've encountered about how life really is. I've been to all 50 of the United States and more than 30 countries due to golf. I feel we are very fortunate to have been born in a place where we can play golf."

Some important steps to understand before getting onto the golf course include how the game is played, how to act on the course, etiquette and rules, the proper dress, arranging to play a round, and the numerous other nuances and intricacies players soak into their minds as they become golfers.

There is so much to comprehend that you're bound to make an error or do something out of turn when you play your first rounds. That's to be expected, and any experienced player who doesn't give you a break isn't doing their part of the learning process. Everyone does something wrong when starting out, and even longtime players aren't immune to making mistakes. Try to take everything in as best you can, and over the course of time, you will become proficient. If you can, try to play most of your golf with experienced golfers so you learn good habits. If you play most of the time with beginners, you may struggle more.

Golf is a natural game

For all its complexities, golf can be simple to play. It all comes down to a player, the course, a set of clubs and the ball. Golf is sport's natural game, played on an open field, forested area, desert, mountains and among lakes and creeks. Upon stepping foot on the course, golfers are usually away from buildings and street noise. Some courses are smack up against busy roads, but most players can enjoy nature's solitude.

A golf course has nine or 18 holes, and its total size is about 130 acres for an 18-hole course. Each hole has a tee, fairway and green. The problem areas to avoid include the rough, bunkers, trees, out-of-bounds and water. Most courses are open to the public. Some are privately owned, others owned by a city, county or state; most resort courses are operated by a company. Private clubs are open only to members and their guests.

Golf is a form of quiet meditation. You can clear your mind of things that have been bothering you and put your attention to playing the game and enjoying the outdoors. The whole experience can be uplifting and ease a person's tensions.

The aerial of Indian River Resort near Stuart, Florida, shows the expansiveness of a golf course—and its peril. A golfer must avoid water, sand and trees to negotiate a course's nine or 18 holes.

Golf is played without much intrusion from any one else. There may be other people to play with, but the golfer is her own referee, counselor and coach. Golf's honor system—recognizing when you've broken a Rule of Golf and calling the penalty on yourself—is perhaps the strongest of any sport. You learn to deal honestly with yourself because if you don't, you cheat yourself of knowing your true abilities, and you may lose your golf friends since no one likes to play with a cheater—one of golf's most-hated words.

Golf is a character builder. From its beginning, it has been a sport of honesty and fair play, a "game for gentlemen and ladies." No matter how good or bad you are, if you follow the rules, you can always find a game.

Your success on the course will, ultimately, be determined in two ways. First, you may play the game for the sheer enjoyment of the outdoors and exercise of walking the course. In that case, you'll find pleasure by striking a great iron shot or rolling in a long putt. Score will not matter to you, but the experience of playing will. Second, you may be analytical and want to measure how well you're doing by score. In that case, you'll be interested in seeing how your score measures up against par, and whether you can be a bogey player, par-shooter, or a par-breaker.

Golf has a lot of do-it-yourself aspects. If you play in its pure form of walking the course, you do a lot of things for yourself: schedule a round, carry your bag, decide playing strategy, make choices on when to gamble, read how putts break, and so forth. Golf is the perfect sport for those independent people who like to make their own playing decisions. These individualistic elements decide a lot of the actions you'll take on the course, from arrival to departure.

How golf is played

Golf is played in groups of players who move around the course after receiving approval to begin play. Most courses don't allow more than four players per group. You can play as a single, twosome or threesome, but expect the first-tee "starter" to join smaller groups together to make a complete group of four. This is done to keep play from slowing down.

Before their first round, new players should have learned how to advance the ball consistently and studied the basic rules and course etiquette (which are covered later in this chapter). Learning both of these will ensure that beginners fit in better with experienced players. Don't embarrass yourself by trying to play on the course before you're ready.

When you're set to play, deciding which course to play is the first part of your adventure. You can either choose to go as a single and hope to be joined with others, or arrange to play with friends. Your group of friends may choose to play the same course all the time, or you may be the experimental types who play as many new courses as possible.

If you're a private-club member, groups usually tee off on a first-come, first-served basis. At public courses, however, you should call ahead to see if you need to reserve a tee time or if groups go off in the order they arrive at the course. In the latter case, a member of your group could arrive early and get in line. However, the other group members need to arrive on time or you'll lose your place. Some courses won't allow groups to be put in line unless every group member is at the course.

If you make a tee-time reservation, a small fee is usually applied. Tee times occur at eight- to 10-minute intervals. The tee time is the time when the first person in your group should be *hitting*. It's not the time for you to arrive at the tee. Get there a few minutes ahead of time. After arranging for a group to play and setting up a time, you must check in at the golf shop in the clubhouse to pay a green fee, settle any other costs such as renting a pull cart, and find out what you need to do to get started on the first hole. In the golf shop, pick up a scorecard, which fits into a pocket and lists the holes, yardages and pars, has spaces to record the scores for each group member, the handicap number to each hole, space to keep track of how the scorekeeper stands in any competitive matches and may have a diagram of the course and the holes individually.

Your arrival time determines whether you want to warm up for the round by hitting practice balls or putts, or if you'll begin play cold, an obvious disadvantage. Whichever you do, you begin play on the first tee, with one exception: groups may be allowed to start on the 10th tee if they can fit in without delaying groups coming off the ninth green. This is a particular practice at a public course. If you do or don't warm up, at least make sure you've stretched your muscles to avoid injury.

The order of play

You decide the order of play—who has the "honor"—within a group in a number of ways. When you're on the first tee it is done by lot, such as:

- Letting a tee fall to the ground; the order of play is decided by who the tee points to each time it is tossed.
- Going from highest to lowest handicaps, or lowest to highest since the better player can guide the other players around.
- Flipping a coin.
- Teeing off according to the set of tees being played, golfers from the back tees (longest) hitting first.
- Odd or even number on the ball (a player guesses if the other players have an odd- or even-numbered golf ball).

♦ By how the names are listed on the scorecard if it's a tournament and the committee made the pairings.

During the playing of the hole, play continues with the golfer farthest from the hole hitting first, even on the putting green. There are some liberties that can be taken in this regard for the sake of speeding play. If players are an identical distance away, the golfer ready to play should go first. In tournaments, a referee may actually measure who is farthest away on the putting green. In casual play, golfers may tap in a short putt if it doesn't need lining up and is not in another player's line of play. And for shots from the rough and fairway, go ahead and play your ball if you're closer than someone who hasn't found hers, then help her find her ball. Only in match play can you be asked to play a shot over if you hit out of turn.

The order of play on every tee except the first is decided by the results of the hole just played. If a par and three bogeys were recorded, the lowest score, the par-shooter, earns the honor. If two players tied for low total, the order between them reverts back to the order of play on the previous hole. If players in a group are using different sets of tees, the same procedure for play should be used for each set of players. And in a two-person team event, the team that wins a hole plays first on the next tee, and those two players can hit in any order they wish.

The tee, or teeing ground, is the starting place for each hole. Players tee off from a designated area indicated by two tee markers, which can be anywhere from 10 to 30 feet apart. The markers define an imaginary rectangular area two club-lengths in depth. The player's ball, not necessarily the golfer, has to be within this rectangle, otherwise she must add two strokes to her score and re-play the shot from within the area.

Object of the game

The object is to hit the ball from the tee to the putting green with your set of clubs and get the ball into the hole in the fewest number of strokes possible. The player is responsible for keeping track of her score on the hole and having it recorded by the player keeping the scorecard. Golfers count every stroke taken, including penalty strokes, to compute the final score.

What constitutes a stroke? Should a swing and miss (whiff) count as one? A miss *is* a stroke because it falls into the definition of a stroke: the forward movement of the club with the intent to hit the ball and move it. If you intended to hit the ball—and here's where honesty comes into play—no matter what happens it's still a stroke. However, you can stop your downswing before the clubhead reaches the ball and it is not considered a stroke.

You'll find that there is an assortment of tees set up at various distances from the green. The tees are usually color coded so that the actual tee markers match with the scorecard. The variety of tees gives the golfer an option of how difficult she wants to make the course. Obviously a set of tees that makes the course play at more than 6,500 yards will be more difficult for a novice player than one at 5,700. You should play the course at a length that matches your playing ability, although there is a tendency to make the game more difficult than necessary from a longer set of tees. Don't let ego get in the way, however, of common sense. Make it a goal to improve enough to move up to the next length as soon as possible. Older courses may not have sets of tees using a color code, but instead have three tee lengths: back, middle and front, or just front and back. The traditional thinking is that the back tees are for expert players, middle for average, and front for juniors, seniors, women and beginners. It's that kind of thinking—of playing tees that suit your ability—that you should use when you play newer courses that have up to seven or eight sets of color-coded tees.

Golfers should also play the course as they find it, with no alterations to the place-

						MATCHES							
BLUE	WHITE	PAR	HANDICAP			+/-	HOLE	+/-			HANDICAP	PAR	RED
496	443	5	8				1				4	5	420
400	386	4	4				2				8	4	349
383	365	4	10				3				12	4	312
125	119	3	18				4				18	3	116
348	339	4	12				5				14	4	309
364	357	4	14				6				10	4	326
290	282	4	16				7				16	4	251
428	412	4	2				8				6	4	376
470	455	5	6				9				2	5	432
3304	3158	37					OUT					37	2891
BLUE	**WHITE**	**PAR**	**HCP**			**+/-**	**HOLE**	**+/-**			**HCP**	**PAR**	**RED**
531	520	5	5				10				1	5	464
419	406	4	3				11				3	4	370
374	357	4	11				12				9	4	322
171	144	3	17				13				17	3	82
404	386	4	7				14				7	4	322
447	432	4	1				15				5	4	371
185	175	3	15				16				15	3	115
359	352	4	13				17				11	4	326
384	374	4	9				18				13	4	319
3274	3146	35					IN					35	2691
6578	6304	72					OUT					72	5582
SCORER											ATTEST		

COURSE RATINGS: Blue 71.3 White 70.2 Red 71.8 SLOPE RATINGS: Blue 120 White 118 Red 120

A typical scorecard shows the hole numbers, yardages for each set of tees, par, handicap holes and has room to keep score and to track the status of any matches taking place. Course and slope ratings are also listed. Most scorecards have a layout of the course, too.

ment of tee markers, hole location or how hazard and out-of-bounds areas are staked. Golfers should simply play the course as it was set up for that day.

Every golfer's goal is to shoot par or better. Par is the score an expert player would be expected to score on a hole, providing conditions are good. An 18-hole course usually has a par ranging from 70 to 76 for women. This is the total of all par scores for the 18 holes added together. Although there is the rare par-6 hole, almost all holes are either a par 3, 4 or 5.

Par 3s are the shortest holes on the course, usually up to 250 yards for men and 210 for women. They are set up so that the player is required to reach the putting green in one shot and take two putts to hole out. Par 4s are longer and take two shots to reach, up to 470 yards for men and 400 for women. And par 5s are the longest holes, usually more than 500 yards for men and 400 for women. It takes three shots for the average player to reach a par 5.

Touching the ball

The Rules of Golf state quite well the amount of freedom a player has in touching the ball. On the teeing ground, the golfer can touch the ball and set it on a tee, or on the ground, to play a shot. She can even move the ball around with her club to find a good lie, as long as the ball stays within the teeing ground boundaries. Once the tee shot is played, however, you normally never touch the ball again until reaching the putting green. You should play the ball as it lies in the fairway and rough, even if it means hitting the ball from an old divot or tall rough.

You can touch the ball during the playing of the hole when the ball comes to rest in casual water or ground under repair (Rule 25 allows you to lift and drop the ball at the nearest point of relief), when it rests in a water hazard (the player may retrieve the ball or drop another when it cannot be played from the water, however, there is a penalty stroke) and when the ball comes to rest so that you may take relief from an obstruction.

A local rule may allow the golfer to lift and clean the ball during muddy conditions.

Leaves are loose impediments. In this situation, with the ball in a hazard (bunker), the leaves can't be moved. Outside of any hazard, however, they can be.

In casual golf, when a course is in poor shape or it is the off-season, players may agree to play "winter rules." There is no such allowance in the Rules of Golf, but for many golfers, playing by winter rules, or "preferred lies," is standard operating procedure. The generic winter rules guideline is that the player can move the ball, on the fairway and fringe areas of the hole she's playing, about six inches, no closer to the hole, to find a more suitable lie. While there is no question that heavy rain, adverse winter weather, and hot, dry stretches can cause enough course damage that finding a good piece of grass is difficult, golfers should avoid playing winter rules unless the course adopts a local rule. Playing the ball as it lies will actually teach you to be a better player, and you'll find that bad lies equal out with good. Beginners, however, might enjoy playing the course more and learn faster if they put the ball on a tee for all their shots, even in the fairway, until they become good at hitting off grass. And to speed play, beginners should pick the ball up as a courtesy to other players when they've taken too many strokes on a hole.

Games golfers play

You'll have an opportunity to play under different formats other than just meeting your regular group for a round of counting strokes. Many of these games involve a wager of some kind, either for a unit of money or a soft drink after the final putts are holed. Here are some familiar competitive contests that will help you enjoy the game in a different way. But remember, if you play one of these games for a wager, pay your bets immediately. That's one of golf's unwritten rules.

- *Match play:* This is golf at its competitive best. An individual or team plays against another individual or team. Hole scores are very important. The side with the lowest score on a hole wins the hole. If a hole is tied, it is "halved"; neither side wins it and it is not carried over to the next hole. The match is over when one side leads by more holes than there are holes remaining.
- *Medal play (also called stroke play):* This is the format under which most people play golf, counting all their strokes. Medal play is a very common format in tournament competition, too. It can be either a team or individual game and last nine, 18, 36, 54, 72 or more holes. The simple goal to win: have the fewest strokes taken. Medal play can be played with gross (actual) scores counting or by using handicap (net).
- *Best ball:* This is a team game that has three possible formats. The lowest score of the team is used, with either no handicap used or handicap included, and done either as stroke play or medal play. The three possibilities: using the best one of two balls, the best one of four, or the best two of four.
- *Scramble (captain's choice):* A fun four-player team game that lets poor players mix in well with better players. All players hit off the tee, then select the best tee ball for their second shot. All players hit a ball from within a couple feet of the chosen ball and select the best shot to play next. This continues until the ball is holed. The scramble is an enjoyable game that often results in low scores. There is a lot of strategy to form teams and decide the order of play within the team.
- *Alternate shot:* A similar game to a scramble, but this time with two players. Both golfers play from the tee and then select the best of the tee shots for the second shot, which is played by the partner whose ball wasn't picked. The players alternate shots until the ball is holed.

Two types of bunkers the golfer is likely to see: Above, the high-lipped bunker requires a lofted shot; below, a flatter bunker allows balls to be putted out in some cases.

- *One-club event:* Great for the off-season, this format has the players selecting just one club to use for the entire round, even for putting. Most players pick a middle iron. This is a wonderful way to teach a golfer how to use her imagination and creativity to play different shots.

- *Skins:* The skins format has become popular since the made-for-television professional Skins Games first appeared in 1983. A skin is one betting unit. A person wins a skin by having the lowest score on a hole; either gross or net scores could be used.

How sides are teamed up in a two versus two contest can be done with some imagination or by the usual method, such as pairing high and low handicappers with two middle handicappers, or flipping a coin, or tossing the four balls in the air on the first tee and teaming the two players whose balls land next to each other.

Some variations include:

Rolling balls to an object such as a tee marker and pairing the two players who do best.

Wait until all four players tee off on the first hole. Then for the first six holes the longest driver teams with the shortest. You repeat the procedure on the seventh tee, but make sure there is a switch. And then on the 13th tee you play with the person you haven't partnered yet.

And if you're playing in a golf cart, you play by the acronym C.O.D., which spells Carts, Opposites and Drivers. The golfers in the same cart play as a team for the first six holes, then the driver of one cart teams with the passenger of the other for six holes, then both drivers play together for the final six holes.

Most of these golf events are played on a handicap or net-score basis, which is your actual score minus your handicap. A handicap is the number of strokes you need subtracted from your actual score to reach a course's U.S. Golf Association course rating, which varies from course to course. Golfers use handicaps so games can be formed with players of various skill levels. A player with a 10-handicap would have to give a 24-handicapper a total of 14 strokes, one each on the Nos. 1 through 14 handicap holes (in other words, the 14 most-difficult holes on the course). If a player receives more than 18 strokes, she would receive one stroke on every hole and two on the number of holes her handicap exceeds 18 starting with the No. 1-handicap hole and counting up.

Playing by the rules

When it comes to golf, the old adage that rules are meant to be broken just doesn't hold up. Without the Rules of Golf, no matter how illogical and unfair they can seem at times, the game wouldn't function very well. Rules give players a frame of reference and a source to go to when something out of the ordinary occurs.

Knowing the Rules of Golf well can be just as important as playing the game well. There are 34 rules, but to explain them takes a 136-page, four-by-six inch booklet. The U.S. Golf Association formulates the rules in conjunction with the Royal & Ancient Golf Club of St. Andrews, Scotland (the two bodies meet every four years—the next meeting is in 1995—to make revisions). There is also a thick supplemental book called the Decisions on the Rules of Golf that goes even deeper into the many situations a player can fall into and what the rulings are.

For instance, a common occurrence is accidentally knocking the ball off the tee while making a waggle. Does that count as a stroke? No, you may re-tee and hit away. What about hitting the ball on a practice swing? Is that a stroke? Not technically, but you have to add a penalty stroke for moving a ball in play and replace the ball to continue. Hundreds of these subtle rulings are included in the primary and supplemental rules books. They make sure both amateurs and professionals adhere to the same playing guidelines, as well as keep the traditions of the game intact.

When the first set of rules was put together in 1744 in Scotland by the Honourable Company of Edinburgh Golfers, there were only 13. Some of them are still observed today, such as playing the entire hole with the same ball and the practice of the farthest person from the hole playing first. Today's rule book, even though it is continually examined for simplification, can be a collection of confusing rhetoric. That's why it's so important to study it. You can obtain a copy for only a couple of dollars by purchasing one at your golf course or by contacting the USGA at Golf House, Far Hills, N.J. 07931, phone 908-234-2300.

After you've studied the book, pack it away in your golf bag. You'll need it by your side when rules decisions are called for on the course. Here's a look at some common rules words and phrases, as well as a summary of things the rules allow and don't allow you to do.

Rules terminology and verbiage

The Rules of Golf has defined numerous terms and words that are used during rules discussions and decisions. Commit them to memory so you can recall them whenever you're involved in a rules discussion.

Addressing the ball: Procedure of player grounding her club and taking her stance in preparation to swing. When in a haz-

Use a rake to smooth out a sand bunker after you've played out of it.

ard, you address the ball when you take your stance only, since you cannot ground your club in a hazard.

Advice: Any conversation that could help a player decide which club to use or how to play a shot.

Ball: Can weigh no more than 1.62 ounces and not measure less than 1.68 inches in diameter.

Ball holed: A ball is holed out after it falls below the level surface of the hole and rests within the circumference of it.

Ball moved: A ball has moved when it moves from its original position and comes to rest in another spot.

Ball in play: As soon as a player makes a swing on the tee with the intent to hit the ball, her ball is considered "in play."

To make a ball drop, hold the ball at shoulder height with your arm extended to the side and let the ball drop straight down.

Ball lost: A ball is considered lost if it hasn't been found within five minutes of the start of a search, or if the player has put another ball in play from where she last played or from where she believes the original ball to be.

Casual water: Temporary gathering of water on the course that can be visible before or after a player takes her stance. Dew and frost are not casual water. The player is allowed to drop away from this area without penalty.

Committee: Group of people in charge of conducting a competitive event; if there is no tournament, the committee is the group of people in charge of the course.

Competitor: Golfer in a stroke-play tournament. A fellow competitor is any golfer the competitor plays with.

Course: Includes the entire area where play is permitted.

Drop: A drop needs to be made after a ball has been lost, gone out-of-bounds or into a water hazard, become unplayable, or is in ground under repair. The drop is made by extending the arm straight out to the side and letting the ball fall from shoulder height.

Ground under repair: Grass or other materials that have been marked by course officials; players are allowed to make a drop away from this area without penalty.

Grounding the club: While in the address position, you ground the club by putting the sole of the club on the surface behind the ball.

Hazard: Any body of water (not casual water) or bunker on the course. You cannot ground the clubhead at address in these areas.

Hole: Also called the cup, this is the lined, round opening on the putting green that is 4 1/4 inches wide and must be 4 inches deep.

The water hazard on the hole is a regular hazard. If the player hit into the water, he or she would have to play their next shot over the water. A lateral hazard usually runs along the side of a hole.

Honor: Playing the first shot on the tee; determined by a coin flip or blind draw on the first tee and by order of lowest score on the other tees.

Lateral water hazard: All or part of a water hazard that makes it impossible to drop a ball to keep the water between the player and the hole; usually marked off with red stakes or lines.

Line of play: Direction the golfer wants the ball to travel during a shot, from where the ball lies to the hole, plus a reasonable area on either side of the intended line.

Line of putt: Direction the player wants the ball to roll after making a putting stroke, plus a reasonable margin on either side of the intended line.

Loose impediments: Natural objects such as stones, leaves, twigs and grass, so long as they are not growing or solidly embedded. Sand and loose soil are such on the putting green; snow and natural ice can be either casual water or loose impediments, at the player's option.

Marker: Person appointed to tally a player's score in a stroke-play tournament.

Observer: An official who accompanies a group and advises on rulings or reports them.

Obstructions: Anything artificial, such as roads and paths, and anything man-made, such as ice. Out-of-bounds fences and markers are not obstructions.

Order of play: Similar to honor; the committee establishes the order of play off the first tee in a tournament.

Out-of-bounds (also called O.B.): Ground that has been disallowed for play, usually bordered by white markers. A shot finishing out-of-bounds must be replayed from the spot of the original shot. Distance is lost and a penalty stroke added, which is the reason for the phrase "stroke and distance."

Outside agency: Anything not part of the competitor's side, including a referee, marker, observer or forecaddie; does not include water or wind.

Partner: Player teamed with another golfer on the same side.

Penalty stroke(s): Added to the score following a rules violation.

Provisional ball: A second ball played from the same spot when an original ball is believed lost outside of a water hazard or may be out-of-bounds.

Referee: Walks with a group to make or assist with rulings.

Relief: A location to drop a ball that rests in a hazard or is affected by an obstruction.

Rub of the green: A moving ball that is deflected or stopped by an outside agency.

Stipulated round: Unless otherwise ruled, a round of 18 holes played in their proper sequential order.

Stroke: Forward movement of the club with the player's intent of hitting the ball.

Teeing ground: Place where play of a hole begins; it is rectangular in shape, two club-lengths in depth, with the front and sides determined by the placement of the tee markers.

Through the green: Entire area of the course except for the tees, putting greens and hazards.

Unplayable lie: Any part of the course, except a water hazard, that the player chooses not to play from. Taking an "unplayable lie" results in a one-stroke penalty.

What you can and can't do

There's really no substitute for reading the actual wording in the Rules of Golf book, but sometimes it is easier to be told what we can and can't do. In general language, here are some common events on the golf course. You can do some of them, and you can't do others. (Many interpretations are taken from the U.S. Golf Association's condensed listing of the rules.)

You can:

- ♦ Mark your ball with dots or other markings to differentiate it from other balls.
- ♦ Replace your ball, without penalty, if it becomes unfit for play, but only on the hole where it became unfit or between holes (Rule 5-3).
- ♦ Accidentally knock the ball off the tee while addressing it, but not count it as a stroke. Replace the ball and play away.
- ♦ Play a provisional ball when you believe your original ball went out-of-bounds or was lost. You are allowed to spend five minutes looking for a lost ball, beginning with the moment you arrive at the area.
- ♦ Mark the ball on the green and wipe it clean before putting. You can do the same thing on the course before full shots only if weather conditions have forced the committee to issue a "lift and clean" rule (Rule 16-1b).
- ♦ Remove loose impediments from the ground around your ball as long as you don't move the ball from its position and it doesn't lie in or touch a hazard (Rule 23-1).
- ♦ Get rid of such man-made things within a hazard as cigars, paper cups and tees.
- ♦ Inquire of another player what the 150-yard markers are or if the hole you're playing is a dogleg par 4 or how long it is. You can ask for any information normally available to the golfers.

- Obtain relief from an obstruction, such as a ball washer or cartpath, without penalty.
- Declare a ball is unplayable if it is in such a position that you can't swing at it. You then lift it, take a penalty stroke and continue playing the hole after taking a drop within two club-lengths of the original spot, not any closer to the hole.
- Be the first to play if you are the farthest from the hole. In teeing off, during match play the winner of a hole tees off first on the next hole; in stroke play, the player with the lowest score on a hole tees off first. If a player plays out of turn in match play at any time, the opponent can ask him to replay (Rule 10-1). In stroke play there is generally no penalty for playing out of turn (Rule 10-2).
- Tee off within two club-lengths behind the front edge of the tee markers. In match play, there is no penalty for playing from outside this area, but your opponent is allowed to make you replay the shot. There is a two-stroke penalty for playing outside this area in stroke play, and you must play from within the correct area (Rule 11-3).
- Make a practice swing, but not a practice stroke, during the playing of a hole. Between holes you may practice chip and putt on or near the putting green of the hole last played or the tee of the next hole but not from a hazard (Rule 7- 2).
- Always play out the hole by holing out, but in match play your opponent may concede your final putt (Rules 3-2, 16-2).
- Replace your ball if it is moved, while at rest, by you, your caddie or partner (except as permitted by the rules), or if it moves after you address it, but you must add a penalty stroke.
- Replace your ball without penalty if it is moved by someone else or another ball while the ball is at rest (Rule 18).
- Play your ball as it lies if your ball in motion is deflected or stopped by another ball at rest. You must add a two-stroke penalty, however, if you're playing stroke play and your ball and another ball were on the green when the two hit (Rule 19-5).
- Re-drop your ball without penalty if a dropped ball hits the player, her partner, caddie or equipment (Rule 20-2a).
- Drop a ball again if a dropped ball rolls into a hazard, out of a hazard, onto a putting green, out-of-bounds or back into the condition from which relief was taken (such as immovable obstructions, abnormal ground conditions and wrong putting green) or comes to rest more than two club-lengths from where it first struck the ground or nearer the hole than its original position or other reference point. If the ball again rolls into such position, place it where it first struck the ground when re-dropped (Rule 20-2c).
- Move movable obstructions found anywhere on the course. If your ball moves, replace it without penalty (Rule 24-1).
- Drop your ball without penalty within one club-length of the nearest point of relief not nearer the hole if your ball is in casual water, ground under repair or, except in a water hazard, a hole made by a burrowing animal. Exceptions are: In a hazard, drop in the nearest position in the hazard that gives maximum relief and is

not nearer the hole or, under penalty of one stroke, drop any distance behind the hazard. On the putting green, place the ball in the nearest position that affords maximum relief and is not nearer the hole (Rule 25-1b).

- Play the ball as it lies in a water hazard, or, adding a penalty stroke, drop any distance behind the water hazard (keeping the point at which the original ball last crossed the edge of the water hazard directly between the hole and the spot on which the ball is dropped). You could just replay the shot (Rule 26-1a,b).
- If your ball goes in a lateral water hazard, drop a ball, with one penalty stroke, within two club-lengths of either where the ball last crossed the hazard edge or at a point on the opposite hazard edge the same distance from the hole (Rule 26-1c).
- Play a provisional ball if you think your ball is lost outside a water hazard or out-of-bounds. You must do so before you move ahead to look for the original, and you must announce your plan. If your original ball turns out to be in a water hazard or is found outside a water hazard, you may not play the provisional ball (Rule 27-2).
- Add a penalty stroke and play the provisional ball if your ball is lost outside a water hazard or is out-of-bounds. If you did not play a provisional, replay the shot (Rule 27-1).
- Add one penalty stroke if you think your ball is unplayable outside a water hazard. Then either drop within two club-lengths no closer to the hole, drop any distance behind the point where the ball lay (keeping that point directly behind the hole and the spot on which the ball is dropped), or replay the shot. If your ball is in a bunker and you elect to proceed under either of the first two options, you must drop in the bunker (Rule 28).

You can't:

- Change the location of the tee markers to where you would like them to be.
- Allow any part of the club to touch the sand in a sand hazard (unless it's indicated to be a waste bunker) or the water and plant growth in a water hazard at address. It is a two-stroke penalty if you do (Rule 13-4).
- Play a round of golf with more than 14 clubs in your bag, including putter and woods.
- Utilize artificial devices that measure distances to the putting green.
- Concede putts to yourself.
- Elect to waive the Rules of Golf for yourself or in agreement with other players in your group.
- Move, from within a hazard, rocks, twigs, pine cones, grass and leaves, or anything natural.
- Inquire about what club a golfer used for a shot or for advice on how to play a shot from the player. You can only get advice from your partner or caddie (Rule 8-1).
- Improve the lie of the ball anywhere on the course, unless weather conditions have forced a local rule to be put into effect.
- Change golf balls during the play of a hole unless it becomes unfit for play.

- Move a loose impediment within one club-length of your ball and have the ball move. You must then replace the ball and add a penalty stroke. On the putting green, there is no penalty stroke as long as the ball moved related to moving the impediment (Rule 18-2c).
- Tap or stamp down spike marks on the green prior to when you putt. You may do so after holing out.
- Play a shot from the out-of-bounds area.
- Move the ball in the fairway with your club during address. It's a penalty stroke if you do.
- Strike the flagstick with your ball while putting on the green.
- Improve your lie, the area of your intended swing or your line of play by moving, bending or breaking anything fixed or growing except in taking your stance or making your swing.
- Push or scrape the ball. Only swing at the ball with the clubhead (Rule 14-1). If your club strikes the ball more than once during the same swing, it counts as one stroke and a penalty stroke (14-4).
- Play a wrong ball, except in a hazard, and not suffer a penalty. In match play, you lose the hole, and in stroke play, you suffer a two-stroke penalty and must play the correct ball (Rule 15).
- Touch the line of your putt (Rule 16-1a). You can't fix spike marks, but you can repair ball marks and old hole plugs in your line before putting (Rule 16-1c).
- Test the putting green by scraping it or rolling a ball (Rule 16-1d).

Etiquette and how to act

Like other sports, golf has its own code of conduct. It's those things you simply do or don't do so that you act properly on the field of play. It's the measure we use to act courteously to others, just as we would want to have them act toward us. Here is a list of procedures—golf's set of Golden Rules—you should do as a golfer to be a friend to the game and to be a compatible playing partner. If you continue to do things that annoy other players, you won't get asked back to play with them. Things you should do include:

- Do leave the course in better shape than you found it when you're done playing, such as repairing divot holes, raking bunkers and picking up trash.
- Do be still and silent when another player is hitting a shot, and stand out of a player's line of sight/peripheral vision. Be careful where your shadow falls. If it crosses a player's putting line or falls on their ball, move out of the way.
- Do avoid stepping up to the tee to hit a shot until the previous player has finished her swing, the ball has come to rest and she has begun to move out of the way.
- Do wait for the players in front of your group to clear out of the way on the fairway or green before your group proceeds. But use common sense. If the group is well out of your range while they putt on the green, don't wait for them to clear off before you hit your approach shot.
- Do fix any damage you see done to the green or fairway, such as divots and ball marks, and rake bunkers when finished. You can't take care of spike marks and unraked bunkers, though, until you've completed play in those locations. Ball marks can be repaired at any time. Walk

lightly on the greens so you don't create scuff marks with your spiked shoes.

♦ Do be prompt when it is your time to play and play without delay. Don't let the group in front of you get more than a half a hole ahead of your group. You should limit your practice swings to one per shot. If your group simply can't stay in contact, and you are being pressured by the following group, let the faster players through. Your group should be the one alert enough to let the next group play through. Ask them to pass you, don't make them ask. The best place to be passed is a par 3. With your group on the green, mark your balls, call for the other group to hit, then stand to the side. Putt out while they approach the green, or wait for them to finish the hole before your group does. A round of nine holes should be played in two hours, and 18 holes in four hours.

♦ Do follow these rules of courtesy on the green: One, be aware of where other balls are on the green and avoid stepping on the line the ball will take to get to the hole. You might make an indentation that affects the roll. Two, mark the ball with accuracy. The best marker is a small coin of a dull color so that it doesn't reflect into a player's eyes. Place the coin exactly behind the ball and as close to it as possible, then lift the ball straight up. Replace the ball in reverse fashion. Three, if your marker is on the same putting line as another player putting from a greater length, offer to move your marker out of the way while the golfer is lining up her putt. You move your marker by finding an object in the distance, such as a tree, in the direction the golfer wants you to move the coin. Put your putterhead alongside the coin extending toward the object; move the coin over. You may need to do this once or twice. Remember to move the coin back before you putt. Four, the player whose ball is nearest the hole should tend the flag for those putting from a greater distance who can't see the hole unless the flag is in it. After everyone has indicated they can see the hole, the flag is put to the side of the green until everyone has putted out. Five, look over your putt to read the break while others are putting—as long as you don't disturb them. This cuts down on the amount of time you'll take when it's your turn. Six, don't lean on your putter when taking the ball out of the hole. It leaves an indentation in the green, especially when the green is wet.

♦ For full shots, do watch the ball roll to a complete stop, especially when you've hit into trouble. Use a marker such as a tree or bunker to help you find the ball so you can go right to it. If you're watching someone hit a shot, watch where the ball ends up, too, so more than one person can locate a wayward shot.

♦ Do put the flagstick back in the hole very carefully in an upright position so you don't damage the cup or the edge. Then unwrap the flag from around the pole so following players can see the wind direction as the flag blows.

♦ If you're a new player, do schedule your times at the course when it will be least crowded. Call the golf shop and see if the course is busy. It can tell you when the fewest number of golfers are present. You will enjoy the game more if you don't feel pressured and rushed by better players.

- Do check around you before swinging. Don't assume everyone knows what you're doing. If you want to practice your swing, don't do it in a crowd. Step away by yourself and everyone will feel safer and stay healthier.

- If your ball sails into a fairway one hole over, do give a warning cry of "Fore!" Then give the players on that hole priority. If they are standing on the tee, wait for them to hit their shots before you step out to play your shot. If they are in the area of your ball, don't play before them unless they let you. If your ball lands on the green of another hole, let the players on that hole play their shots to the green or finish putting, whichever applies. Then you can retrieve your ball and drop it on the fringe area, no closer to the hole you are playing.

And now for the things you should not do so you don't damage the course or cause a disruption in play with your playing partners.

- Don't let any riding or pull carts get taken near tees and greens. Follow all directional signs for these pieces of equipment. Tees and greens have short-cut grass and the tires on a cart can do damage that takes time to disappear. Find out in the golf shop whether carts must be kept on paved paths. Don't park cars in front of a green. Park cars and carts behind the green in the direction of the next tee.

- Don't leave the putting green area for the next tee until your playing partners have finished putting. You are playing as a group so you should go around the course as a group. If you feel the other players are going too slow, say something to them. Don't try to speed up play by yourself. You'll appear rude rather than speedy.

- Don't place your golf bag on the green or tee. Put it on the fringe or to the side of the tee.

- Don't walk or stand ahead of a player in your group who is playing a shot. It is okay to walk to your ball while someone is getting ready to hit, but not if it is a couple hundred yards down the fairway. The entire group should move along quickly as one unit.

- Don't turn your body to face toward where a warning cry of "Fore!" came from. You're likely to get struck in the front by the ball. Instead turn your back to where the ball will come from and cover your head so your back or legs take the blow, not your head and face.

- Don't walk up to a golfer from behind while he or she is making a practice swing or setting up to hit the ball. They won't see you coming and shouldn't be expected to avoid hitting you.

- Don't swing your club toward someone. You may send flying debris at them, or in an unlikely event, your club could slip from your grip or the clubhead come off. Make sure you have a clear area in front of you before swinging.

- Don't automatically hit another ball after you have hit one out-of-bounds off the tee. Wait for the other group members to play their first shots before hitting your next one.

- Don't hold a conversation with someone while another golfer is getting set to hit a shot, unless it's a whisper. If a discussion is in progress, put it on hold until everyone has teed off.

- Don't give swing tips or comments to anyone unless they ask you for them or if it's been arranged ahead of time.
- Don't lose your cool if you're the player keeping the scorecard. Stay level-headed so you can keep track of everyone's score properly and keep the tally on any competition going on.
- Don't stroke a putt over again right away after you've missed one. Just like the rule for hitting a ball out-of-bounds, wait for everyone to finish the hole then hit the putt over again, but only if there's no one waiting on you in the fairway.
- Don't tell a player they've hit a great shot while the ball is still in the air. Wait to give a compliment until you see the total result of the shot. A ball that appears to be good in flight may be affected by wind or a strange bounce when it lands. Saying "Great shot" too early will make you look silly when the ball ends up poorly.

Some rules of safety

A golf course is usually a very safe place to be. The likelihood of you getting hurt is very slim, and there's more chance of getting hurt while walking up and down stairs in the clubhouse than of getting hit by a golf ball.

The golf course can be a dangerous place in two areas. The first is severe weather. The second is in operating a riding cart. Here are some safety tips to follow for both.

Lightning can be a killer, plain and simple. When you see lightning in the area, or hear thunder no matter how distant, follow these safety tips:

1. Get off the course immediately (you are within your rights to leave the course at any tournament).
2. Rush to a dense, wooded area. Avoid isolated trees.
3. When caught in the open, fall to your knees and tuck your head.
4. Take off your spiked golf shoes.
5. Get rid of your umbrella, even if it has a fiberglass shaft.
6. Stay away from your golf clubs and never get caught holding one.
7. Get as far away from ponds or lakes as possible.
8. Remember: golf carts are not a safe haven.
9. Avoid the putting green.
10. Get to the clubhouse as fast as you can. There really is no other safe haven on the course besides the clubhouse.

As for riding carts, observe all the safety rules posted at the course. Drive on paths only if you can. Only operate the cart from the driver's side, and have no more than two players in the cart at the same time. Don't move the cart while someone is hitting a shot nearby because the noise of the engine and rattling of clubs will be heard. Make the use of a cart effective by dropping off a player at her ball and then going over to your's so she can be hitting while you get ready for your shot.

You'll find a sticker, required by law, on the cart that explains how to operate it and some things you should and shouldn't do to enjoy it safely. As much as a riding cart looks like something fun to play with at an amusement park, people have been injured by overturned carts or carts out of control going down steep hills. Read the driving instructions in the cart, and try to avoid sudden turns that can throw a passenger out. Also, drive straight up or down a hill, not along slopes.

The thrill of golf lasts all year in all conditions, even after the autumn season, when most players in the country take a break from the game.

5 The Full Swing, Getting It Right

What golf means to: Amy Alcott, LPGA star player. "Golf has given me an arena to showcase my creativity. It's also perfectly suited to my personality. It brings out the gentle side in people. It brings out the anger in people. I'm very much a loner, but I'm also a people person. In golf, you're either playing real good or not good. It's a black-and-white sport. It doesn't have much gray area."

By now your head may be swimming with too much information, and you haven't even read one word about how to swing the club! There is an awful lot to take in, but when learning the swing itself, try to keep things as clear in your mind as possible.

A simple way to start learning the swing is to realize that you will build a swing, piece by piece. You shouldn't try to learn it all at once. You haven't experienced confusion until you take up a club and try to make a full swing without learning all the basics. The swing must be learned in sections. The final goal is to swing with one continuous motion, but during the learning stage you focus on the swing as pieces of a puzzle to fit together. You learn the fundamentals first, such as grip, stance and posture, and build the rest of the swing upon them. If you learn the basics well initially, then you will have an easier time of adding the more difficult parts.

Everything starts with the grip

One thing most players pay too little attention to is the grip. It's amazing how critical the grip is when compared to bigger parts of the swing such as arm movements, shoulder turn and hip turn. But if you think about it, it makes perfectly good sense. The grip is the only connection we have to the club, which is what strikes the ball. If the grip is done poorly, you can have the prettiest swing and still experience problems with getting the ball to go straight. With a bad grip, you have to compensate in other parts of the swing to make it work. When all parts of the swing and set-up aren't correct, you fight a continual problem with inconsistency.

From the start, you must resist the urge to grip the club in whatever way feels most comfortable. As unreasonable as it seems, comfort isn't necessarily what you need. The correct grip may feel uncomfortable at first, but the more you play, the better it will feel. Stick with it. You'll be rewarded for years to come with a sound grip.

To grip correctly, stand straight and have a club leaning against the front of your left thigh (most instructions in this book will be for right-handers; lefties will have to reverse directions). Let your arms hang naturally by your side. You must be careful on this point,

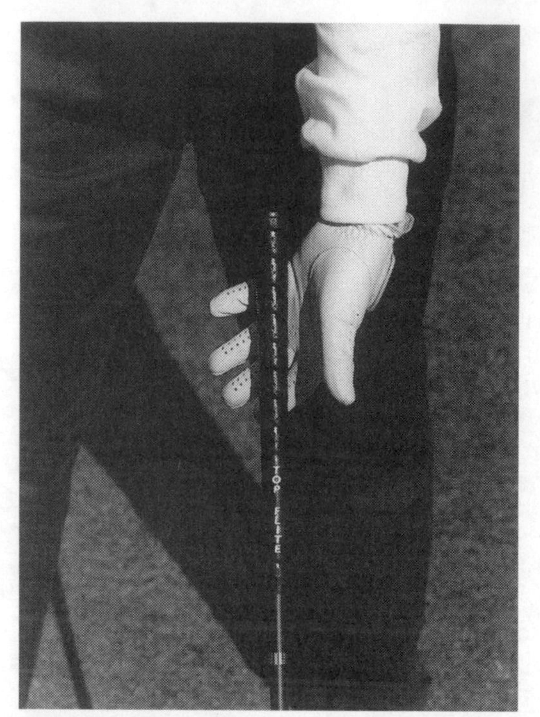

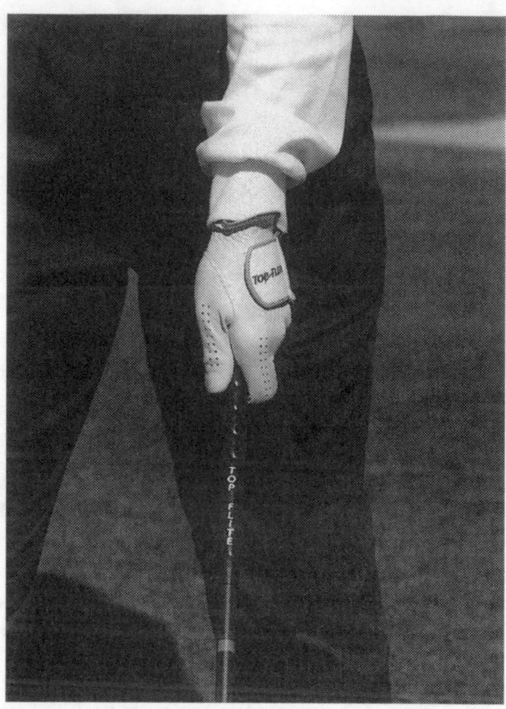

The grip begins with the left hand going on first (top left), with the grip going diagonally across the fingers. The hand closes over the grip (top right) so that the thumb is on the right side of the grip (below).

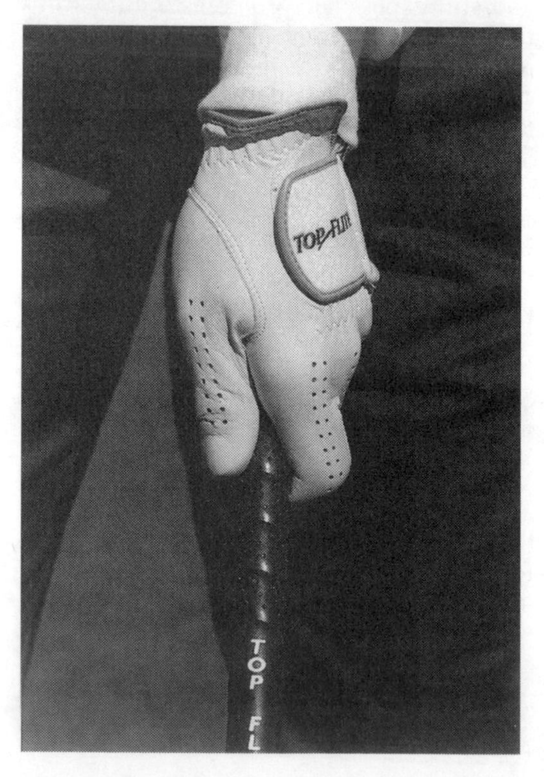

as it is natural for some women to stand with the inside creases of the elbows facing outward. You want to stand with the elbow folds almost completely facing the sides of the body. Standing in this position, move the left hand onto the club near the top of the grip. Let the hand go on naturally without changing the angle of the arm as it hangs.

The full-swing grip should be held more in your fingers of both hands, not your palms. (For putting, the grip is held in the palms.) If you open your left hand, you'll see that the grip runs diagonally from the base of the little finger to the middle joint of the index finger. With your hand closed, the left thumb should be slightly right of center on top of the grip.

You put your right hand on the club to complete the grip. Hold onto the club with your left hand and bend your arms at the elbow. Stretch your arms in front of you, with the forearms parallel to the ground. Put

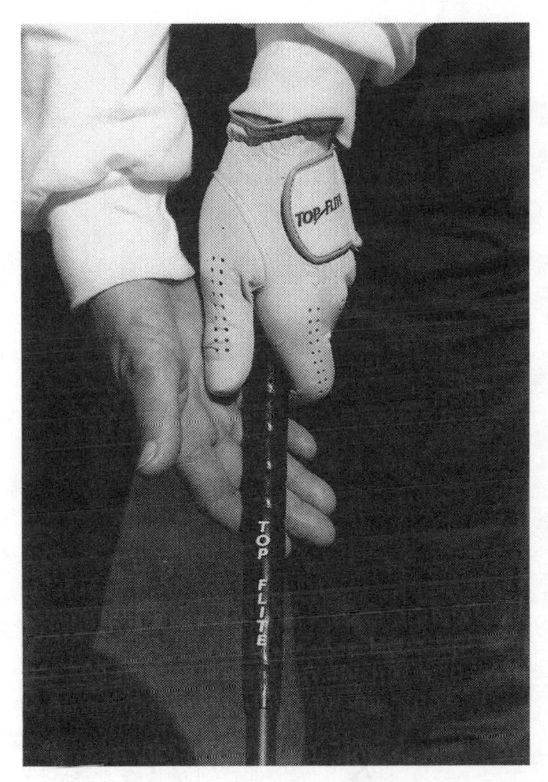

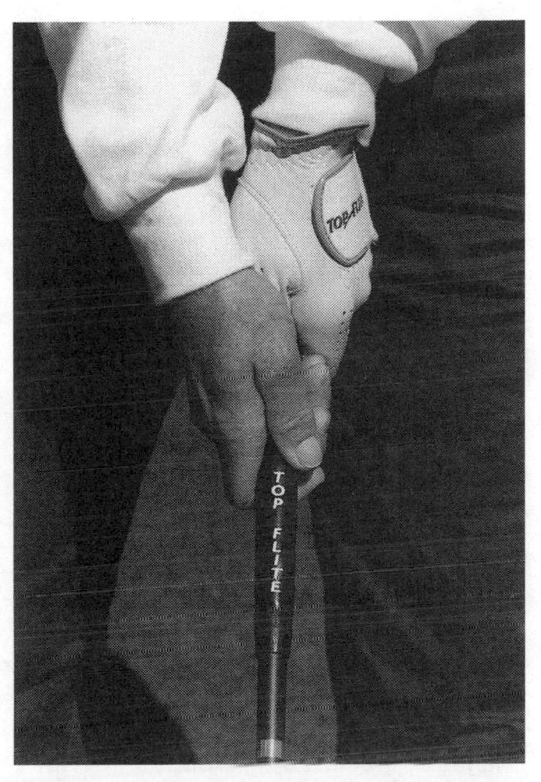

The right hand goes on the club so that the thumb pad fits over the thumb of the left hand. The "Vs" formed by the thumb and forefinger of each hand point toward the right side of the face.

your right hand on the club and slide it up snugly with the left hand. The right hand fits on the club so that the thumb pad of the right hand sits on the top of the left thumb, the lifeline of your right hand goes against the right side of the left thumb, the right little finger wraps around the groove between the first two fingers of the left hand, and when the hand is closed, the right thumb sits slightly left of center on top of the grip.

This kind of grip is the overlap (or Vardon) grip, which is best for golfers with large hands. This is the most common of three types of grips. The other two are the interlock, in which the little finger of the right hand intertwines with the index and middle fingers of the left, and the full-finger or baseball grip. For the full-finger grip, all fingers are wrapped around the club and the hands don't hook together at all. The interlock is ideal for people with small hands, and the baseball grip is best for beginners and weaker players because the hands have more control and contact with the club. If you're a beginner, try the full-finger grip until you're consistent, then switch to one of the other two grips.

A final grip check includes looking in a mirror to see that the "Vs" formed on both hands by the index fingers and thumbs point toward the right side of the face. Lower the clubhead end of the club to the ground so these "Vs" are clearly visible. With your hands in these positions, you have a neutral grip, designed to set the clubhead up to the ball squarely at the address position and during impact. This is the grip to use for all your full-swing shots. If you use this grip with a light pressure, just enough so that the club can't be pulled out of your hands, it will let your wrists and hands hinge properly during the swing.

The three types of grips most often used are the interlocking (above left), overlap (above right) and baseball or full-finger grip (below).

How to address the ball

With your correct grip, the next stage is to step up into the proper posture position, the last step before the swing motion. This is a four-step procedure appropriately called "Getting into the address position." It's done in this manner: First, stand in a relaxed posture with your arms hanging by your side and the club in your left hand. Second, follow the procedure for putting your right hand on the club for the proper grip. Third, lower the club and bend from the hips at the same time, stopping when the clubhead is a foot or less above the ground. Fourth, flex your knees so they feel relaxed and springy. That will lower the clubhead the rest of the way until it touches the ground.

This is the starting position to the swing. With continual practice, not only will you put your hands on the club in quick fashion and correctly, you will learn to assume the address position in a matter of seconds, with little cause to think through the process step

Get into the address position by properly gripping the club and holding it in front of you.

by step. The entire procedure will become second nature. You should have the sensation of flexing the knees, as if you were going to sit on a high stool.

To make sure you've done the position correctly, you'll want to check that these other factors were done right. Your back should be straight, your shoulders not rounded, body weight evenly balanced on both feet, your shoulders lined up over the knees and middle of your feet, the spine tilted slightly right since the right hand is lower than the left, the right foot perpendicular to the target line, left foot turned outward at a slight angle, and right elbow lower than the left. Wow, got all that? It seems like a lot, but if your knees are flexed, rear end out and club resting on the ground, all of these checkpoints should take care of themselves.

The pre-shot routine

In later chapters you'll read about changes to the basic address position in order to hit specialty shots. For now, though, in order to learn the swing, you will need to set up for a straight shot in the square position.

Grip, posture and alignment are all parts of every pre-shot routine. You've learned grip and posture. To line up yourself and the clubface to the intended target, consider how a football kicker and a pool player line up. They stand behind the ball, imagine a line from the ball to the target (the target line), then locate a spot on that line they want the ball to travel over. In golf, it's the same way. Stand behind the ball after picking out the club you're going to hit. Imagine a line drawn from the ball to your target. About three feet on the other side of the ball, pick out an object you can use as a directional aid. It could be a dead spot in the grass, or an old tee, or some other kind of blemish. Keep that spot in sight as you move to the side of the ball. Place the clubhead behind the ball so the clubface lines up with the spot you've picked out. By doing this you know the club is lined up square with the ball and target. Step in with the right foot as you line up the clubface. When everything is set, put the rest of your

The next step is lowering the club (above left) and then flexing your knees to get the club to the ground (top right). Below is the address position with the driver.

body in the address posture. Make sure your entire body is parallel with the target line. To check this for correctness, picture three lines that join your shoulders as one unit, hip joints as one and heels as one. If these three lines are parallel with the target line, then you're lined up properly. This is called having everything in the square position.

Ball position is the phrase used to describe how the ball is situated in relation to your feet. For most shots, the ball will be off the left side of your face. If you drew a hash mark to indicate the middle spot between your feet, the proper ball position would be to the left of center to correspond with the ball off the left side of your face. Play the ball in this position for all shots, except the special shots explained later and for fairway woods and the driver. For those longer clubs, play the ball off your left armpit.

The three-step process to aim the club includes lining up the shot from behind the ball and picking an aiming point on line with the flag (above left). Step up to the ball with the right foot first and sole the club (above right). And finally, bring the left foot in so that your feet, knees, hips and shoulders are lined up toward the target (below right).

Swinging the club, the mini-swing

The nucleus of the swing is the mini-swing, the portion that contains the swing's potential for power, accuracy and performance. The club is released into the ball during the nucleus. Provided this release takes place at the right moment, and the clubface strikes the ball on the center of the face, you will experience maximum distance and accuracy.

Anyone who plays the game with expertise does the mini-swing portion well. It's what sets professionals apart from amateurs. Specifically, the mini-swing is the middle portion of the full swing. It has a half-backswing and half-forward swing, similar to the partial shot you'll learn in Chapter 10. The mini-swing has everything you need for a good swing: a backswing that builds power, a downswing that returns the clubface squarely to the ball, and a follow-

The mini-swing motion: The player swings the club until the hands are waist high (top left) and the clubshaft points at or inside of the ball (top right) on the backswing; the impact position (bottom left) and follow-through (bottom right) release the club and transfer the body weight. The body faces the target on the follow-through (opposite page).

through that culminates the release of power and has the golfer finishing balanced and facing the target.

Beginning golfers should at least perform the mini-swing well before heading out to the golf course. It's an excellent way to make sure you can advance the ball down the fairway with regularity.

Learn the mini-swing by first getting into the address position just discussed. With a 5- or 6-iron in your hands, swing the club back with your arms, shoulders and hips moving at the same time. The left side of the body keys the start of the backswing, with the left arm and leg turning at the same time as you smoothly take the club back. Don't watch the clubhead as it moves. Focus on the ball and move the club back by extending, not stretching, your arms.

Stop swinging when your hands reach chest high. Your left arm should be straight and parallel with the ground, your left wrist flat, your weight moved to the right leg and the club pointing upward. To be precise, the clubshaft should be pointing at the target line. In fact, if you were to imagine the target line continuing on the right side of the ball, you would want to make sure the shaft of the club points at some point on that entire target line or is parallel to it during the swing.

From this halfway position on the backswing, begin to swing down by shifting your weight to the left side with your left leg. Your arms and shoulders start turning toward the left immediately after the left leg has started to turn back to the left. As your left arm pulls the butt end of the club down and through, try to maintain the angle of the clubshaft and arms you created at the end of the backswing. Hold that angle for as long as possible to release energy at the last moment. Make this all a smooth movement, however. Don't try to consciously let your hands release the club. Your arms and hands must work freely. Visualize returning the clubface back to the position it was in at address. Finish the mini-swing by letting the force of the swing turn your body to face the target. Your right arm should be parallel with the ground, the right hand should have passed over the left after impact, the clubshaft should be pointing upward and at the ball-target line, and your weight should be on the left. Stop swinging when your hands are chest high on the left side of your body. Your right knee should be bent with the leg balanced on the toes.

Going the final step

You will probably have the desire to jump the gun on the learning time-period needed to feel comfortable with the swing. This is particularly true with older beginners. There's an impatience that is hard to overcome. The older we are, the more we get tied up with having to see immediate

Once the mini-swing is learned, the full swing is a matter of increasing the amount of body turn back (top left) and through (bottom). Just after impact (top right) the head remains steady as body weight moves to the left side.

results. That's why golf is best learned as a junior.

However, many of us don't have that option. So when we learn as adults, we have to be extra patient. You've just learned about the mini-swing. Practice this motion for many hours, making dozens of swings, either with or without a ball in front of you. It would probably be best to swing without a ball for the early stages, since it could be expensive to run through range balls at such a quick rate. Swing for a month or more before ever hitting a ball. It's the easiest way to learn. Learn the proper motions and just swing. When you're ready to hit a golf ball, you won't have any bad habits. There are a number of ways to practice this movement so that your golf muscles are toned up.

If you can, make the swing motion in front of a full-length mirror so you can see how things are working. On sunny days, swing with the sun to your back and watch your shadow, again looking for accuracy in duplicating swing movements. One of legendary teacher Harvey Penick's favorite drills was the slow-motion drill, in which students make swings in slow motion for easier coordination of arms and legs. Stop at certain moments, such as the top of the swing and impact, to look at where your arms and legs are positioned.

If you invest in a hitting net, the money you'd spend would eventually be saved in not having to go to the practice area. Set up the net in your yard and you can have the convenience of practicing whenever time allows.

An excellent way to stay flexible and learn the swing movement is to take your driver, a broom handle or an exercise bar and put it behind your back along the shoulder blades. Stand in the address position with your knees flexed. Now make a backswing turn so that one end of the object you're turning points at the ball. Turn the other way so the other end points at the ball. Do this 10 times to the right and 10 to the left each day and you'll feel flexible in your upper body and learn how the swing motion feels.

You complete the full-swing picture by enlarging the mini-swing. You simply make a longer backswing and follow-through. Imagine that the backswing is the calm before the storm. You're loading up power and energy as you wind around your upper body, using your hips and legs as anchors. If all works well, the downswing lets all that power release at just the right time to strike the ball for maximum accuracy and distance.

After getting into the address position, the backswing is finished by continuing to turn beyond the mini-swing position. The stopping point is when you feel your shoulders have turned 90 degrees and your hips 45. This is the top of the backswing. At this point, check that your left knee points at or just to the right of the ball, the club is parallel with the ground and pointing toward the target, your shoulders and back are turned behind the ball, your right hand is over the right shoulder, and your back is facing your aiming point.

Your left heel may or may not be off the ground at the top of the swing. If you are flexible, it's a good idea to keep the heel planted. It keeps you in control, eliminates extra movement, and gives you a firmer foundation. If your heel has to come up, that's not all that bad either, as long as your left leg hasn't spun so far to the right that the foot is balanced on the toe. No less than half of your left foot should still be grounded. With the left heel up, you can make a bigger shoulder turn and, in theory, hit the ball farther. Whether you plant or lift the left heel, you need to make sure you transferred your weight from a balanced position to the right side on the backswing.

The action of the head has long been debated. It used to be that "keep your head still" was everyone's motto. But today it's felt that keeping the head rock solid still can cause a reverse weight shift, meaning your weight doesn't transfer over to the right and hangs over on the left side. It's okay for the head to move somewhat to the right on the backswing, as long as it doesn't go past its position at address until well past impact. It's natural for the head to move because the shoulders and upper body are turning away from the ball.

Most teachers used to insist on a rigidly straight left arm from the address position until the follow-through. But like head movement, there's been some revisionist thinking about the arm. It's okay to have a slight bend in the left arm at the top of the swing, but if you're flexible enough not to bend it, then don't. The left arm should be straight, however, at address and impact.

Ready to release power

Now that you're coiled at the top of the swing, you're ready to release all that energy, which is the purpose of the downswing. The downswing occurs at a much quicker rate than the backswing in order to release the power of the swing. If you swung the club down as slowly as you swung it back, your "powder-puff" swing wouldn't send the ball very far. Because of the quickness of the downswing, it's important that you initially do this portion in practice as slow as possible, without a ball, to get a feel for it. Gradually build speed until you feel comfortable, then begin hitting shots.

The downswing actually begins just as the club is nearing the top of the swing. The left foot stabilizes and "grabs" the ground as an anchor. The left knee moves to the left, getting the entire left side ready to receive the transfer of body weight from the right side. The hips are also turning to the left, working with the left leg to unwind the lower body. Secondary to this lower body movement, but occurring as a result of it, is the action of the shoulders and arms, which pull the club downward. The wrists remain cocked as they were at the top of the swing.

The left side of the body continues to rotate to the left, bringing body weight to the left as the hips open up. The shoulders and arms have continued to rotate around, with the right shoulder moving under the chin. The wrist cock straightens out as the hands reach the bottom of their arc, releasing the club for the precise moment of impact to the ball.

At impact, the club and golfer should be in virtually the same position they were at address. The shaft should lean forward, the left wrist should be flat, and the left shoulder should be higher than the right. In addition, the hips should be open about 45 degrees, the shoulders should be square to the ball-target line but ready to open, the arms have straightened, the wrists have uncocked, and the clubface is square to the ball.

Swing to the finish

If you have done things properly up to the impact position, then there's little else you need to do to finish a correct swing. Things will happen pretty much without your extra effort. After impact, you want to feel as though you are swinging the club down the target line as long as possible as the body continues to unwind to the left. This extension movement allows all your power to be released and keeps you from pulling your body to the left or pushing the body more to the right. Either one of those movements would make the ball go off-line. You can learn to extend the club by swinging a 5-iron with your right arm only, putting your left behind the back. Choke down on the club with your right hand and make a swing as you would if you were using two hands.

The swing culminates as you bring the arms out, around and up, with your hands finishing by the back of your head or around the left ear. Your body should now be facing the intended target and most of your weight on the left leg. The right leg carries practically no weight and the right foot is balanced on the toe.

That completes the entire swing movement that professionals make with such ease but beginners struggle with for so long. But with patience, diligence and an eye for details, you can learn to swing consistently well and enjoy the benefits of a good long game.

SAVING STROKES WITH THE SHORT GAME

What golf means to: Patty Berg, LPGA Hall of Fame member. "There isn't anything I don't like about golf. It gave me the opportunity to travel all through the United States, to meet wonderful friends, to stay in sports after growing up with football and ice-skating. And most of all, it gave me the opportunity to match my talent against people all over the world."

Nothing can make your score soar like shots you've frittered away from 80 yards in. Three-putting can be a hole killer, but there's always the potential for a one- or two-putt to save your score. The shots that really pile up in a hurry, though, are the ones from close range. These are the shots made with your high-lofted clubs, such as the 9-iron and wedges, that make up a player's short game. If you are adept in this area, look out world. You will likely become a strong player because you'll always have the potential for a hot hand. If you're a good short-game player, it's likely you will have good touch with the putter, too. But if you lack skill around the greens, you can't expect to ever be better than a mediocre player.

That's a harsh statement, but let's face it, you're not always going to hit greens in regulation. If you're a beginner, probably half of the shots you play during a round will be from 50 yards and closer. So you need to develop a good short game to make up for being inaccurate with the longer clubs. The short game, though, provides many players with headaches. You need to develop a sense of feel for playing these touch shots. The short game presents obstacles of having to hit three-quarter shots, shots over trouble, low shots, shots along the ground, and a host of other plays that have to be done through feel. The player must gauge, with imagination, how to play a short shot, deciding how hard to hit the ball, with what kind of trajectory, where to land it, and then pull it off.

There are similar problems with shots out of sand, which is just as much a problem spot for golfers as shots around the green. The unpredictability of how sand will react when hit puts fear into the uneasy player, causing her to hit fat and thin shots. Adding the wasted shots from around the green with two or three extra shots taken from a bunker will give you a high handicap.

In this chapter, you'll learn the proper technique to playing chips, pitches and sand shots so that you can, with a relaxed attitude, execute the shots as successfully as you'd planned and visualized them.

Mastering the short game

To play an assortment of shots around the greens, you have to understand what clubs you can use and how they function. As mentioned, you'll play most short-game shots with your high-lofted clubs, but actually, every club in your bag has the potential to be used for a chip or pitch. A chip is any shot played from the short grass around the green known as the fringe, apron or collar, and it usually has a low ball flight. A pitch is from a greater distance with a higher ball trajectory.

For shots around 80 yards, most women use a 9-iron. And as you learned in Chapter 3 about equipment, there are a variety of wedges with different lofts. A conventional pitching wedge, with 50 degrees of loft, would be used for 70-yard shots, and a standard sand wedge (55 degrees) for 50-yarders. Wedges with more loft than a regular pitching wedge will hit the ball shorter. So examine the clubhead to see how many degrees are listed on it and, when you feel you're ready to expand from a pitching and sand wedge, add it to your set. With the number of options now available for golfers to play around the greens, it really benefits you to have at least three wedges. Take another club out of your bag that you don't use very much, such as a long iron or fairway wood, to add a wedge and stay within the 14-club limit.

Wedges are for pitch shots from the fairway or high shots over bunkers, trees and water. They can be used around the green, too, but when the ball is on the fringe, you could also use a putter, or a 7-iron through 2-iron. Your short-game options are many, which is reason enough for you to practice these shots as often as possible to know how each club can help you in different situations. There are probably two universal rules you can count on. First is that any time your ball is sitting low in high grass, play your most-lofted club. The second deals with the hardness of the ground the ball is sitting on. The softer the ground, the harder you should swing. The harder the ground, the softer the swing should be.

Three basic pitch shots

You need to make adjustments in your posture, stance and ball position to hit a pitch shot. There are three types of pitches, different by the trajectory of the ball. The more you play and practice, the more you'll become accustomed to the length of backswing needed to hit the ball certain distances with certain ball flights. The lie of the ball plays a big role in determining the type of shot you play. The better the lie is, the more it sits up on the grass, the easier the shot will be. Analyze your situation, examine the turf conditions and go on experience when deciding how to play a pitch. Usually a lower shot is the safest bet, giving the ball minimum air time and maximum ground time. A low shot gets the ball on the ground faster so that it can roll to the hole. Most people have an easier time judging how hard to roll something rather than how hard to make it fly the correct distance.

Three types of shots can be played with a pitching wedge. You play the *run shot* when there is no trouble in front of the green and the flag is in the middle, or if the flag is toward the back of the green. The ball has a low flight and will roll a long way upon landing. The *walk shot* is best played to a flag positioned in the middle or back of the green since the ball will roll a short ways after a medium-height ball flight. And the *sit shot* should be played when there is very little green to land the ball before the flag. Usually this happens when the flag is in the front of the green or just beyond a bunker or hazard. You can also play the shot over a tree. The ball flies very high and lands softly, only rolling a few feet. The sit shot could be played with any of the multi-lofted sand wedges, but only if the lie is good.

The *run shot* is played by narrowing your feet together and pulling the left foot

The run shot: Begins with body weight on the left side and hands ahead of the ball (top left); the legs remain quiet on the backswing (top right); at impact (bottom left) the hands have led the clubhead, which stays low on the follow-through (bottom right).

back off the target line to open the stance. Play the ball in the middle and have most of your weight on the left side. Aim the clubface square to the target. Swing the club back smoothly, moving the arms and shoulders together. Your lower body is very "quiet." Your wrists should hinge up. Hold that wrist angle on the downswing as long as possible. Let the club land on top of the ball, pinching it against the turf. Keep the hands moving so that they lead the clubhead at impact. Let your hands finish at waist or chest high. The ball will fly like a line drive in baseball and run for many yards.

The *walk-shot* swing is played very much like a regular pitching wedge. The ball reacts the same way, too, flying with a normal, medium height, landing softly and rolling a short distance. Square your feet and the clubface with the target line. Play the ball off your left heel and balance your weight evenly on both legs. Again, you should have little leg movement during the shot. Swing your hands back until they are about waist high. The club should point upward, making an L-shape with the arms. Don't swing down as sharply as you did for the run shot, but hit the ball with a descending blow. The club's loft will lift the ball. Complete the shot with a mirror image of the backswing, the arms at waist high, the club pointing up and the body facing the target. Don't overswing for this or any short shot. Just keep your body moving, and if you swung correctly the ball will fly nicely.

The *sit shot* is struck just the opposite of the run shot, and you get contrasting results, too. The sit shot is the trickiest of the three to play. First, you need to have a good lie. If the ball is sitting down, don't try it. Second, because the arc of the swing is U-shaped, there is very little margin for error at the bottom where you make contact with the ball. If you don't time it precisely, you'll hit the ball fat or thin. And third, you need to use a sand wedge, a club you won't be as familiar with on grass as in sand. Open your stance more than you did for the run shot. Also open the clubface so it appears to be aimed slightly right of the flag. Play the ball off the left heel and have your weight evenly placed on both legs. With a light grip pressure, swing the club back along your stance line. The club will swing out away from you. Let the hands get to chest high, then swing the club on the same path coming down, following the stance line. The club will swing down and across the target line and finish to the left of you. Finish with the hands chest high and the club pointing upward, with the wrists hinged and your body facing the target. The ball will have a lot of height to it, land softly and roll a short ways.

Other short-game special shots

The run, walk and sit shots will be the main weapons in your short-game arsenal, but there are a couple of other shots to help you in other situations.

The *Texas wedge* is not a wedge at all, but the use of the putter away from the green. When you're in a situation with the ball up to 30 feet off the green and the grass is cut short and smooth, you might feel more comfortable hitting the putter instead of a lofted club. (Bumpy, thatchy grass will knock the ball off line.) Your goal isn't to make the "putt" but to get the ball close to the hole, the same goal you have with a short-iron chip. With the Texas wedge you worry about how hard to hit the ball, not where to land it. Line up the shot as you would a putt, allowing for the proper amount of break. Play the shot from your putting posture, perhaps standing a little more upright, with your regular putting grip. Instead of a smooth stroke, however, hit the ball with a jabbing motion so the ball skips over the grass. By the time the ball gets to the green, it will start rolling like a putt. The key to how hard to hit the ball is picturing how hard you would need to hit the ball from the edge of the green to the hole, then apply a third or a quarter more power behind the stroke.

The walk shot: Weight is balanced on both feet to begin the shot (top left). The club points upward on the backswing as the wrists hinge (top right). At impact, the hands have again led the club, letting the loft of the face lift the ball (bottom left). The follow-through (bottom right) duplicates the backswing.

The sit shot: The left foot is pulled back from the stance line at address (top left). The club is going along the stance line away from the body (top right), and swings along that same line on the downswing, cutting across the ball (bottom left).

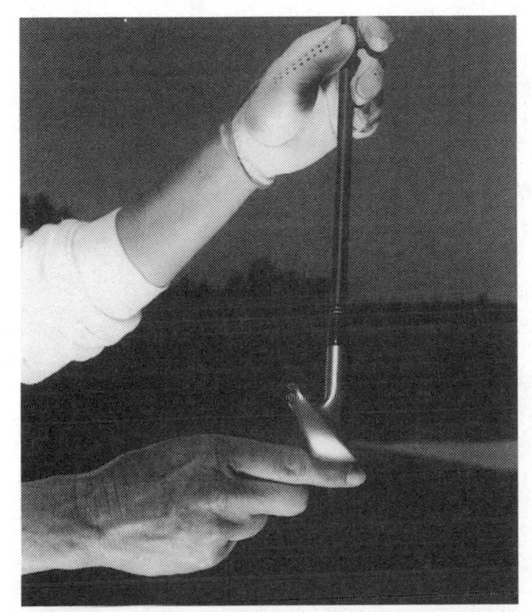

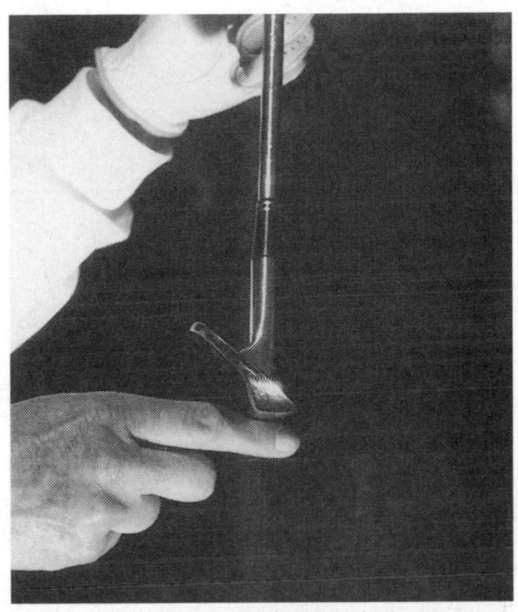

A pitching wedge (left) doesn't have as much bounce as a sand wedge (right). The flange of the sand wedge lets it sweep through sand rather than dig into it.

When the ball is just three to five feet off the green, a great play is to hit a *low, running shot*. You might be tempted to use your putter in this case, but do so only if the grass is short and smooth. That way you will have a better chance of judging the speed of the shot. In taller grass, however, with a level lie, chip the ball with a 7- or 8-iron (for long shots up a slope, use a medium or long iron; for downhill shots, play a pitching or sand wedge). Line up the shot like a putt, playing the break, because this shot could be holed out. Play the ball more toward your back, or right, foot and move your weight forward onto the left leg. Move your hands forward, too, toward the target and ahead of the ball. Then swing the club with a pendulum motion, not letting your wrists break. Only take the club back a short way, as much as you think will get the ball to finish by the hole, and accelerate the club through impact. Strike the ball at the bottom of the swing arc. The ball will fly low, clear the fringe and roll like a putt.

Both past and present course architects have made use of mounds or humps in the putting green. In some cases your ball will be short of the green and you'll have to play a shot to a flag just beyond one of these mounds. You wouldn't want to fly a shot to the hole because it would bounce off the mound and be uncontrollable. The best shot is to either play a Texas wedge, or use a 6-iron and hit a bump-and-run shot. For the latter, position yourself as you would for a shot on the fringe with a 7-iron and aim to have the ball roll up the closest side of the mound to you to the top and then go over to the other side as it slows down. Swing the club back low for a few feet and then pop the ball up to land close to the mound.

You'll encounter many other situations around the greens that call for you to creatively plan a shot to get the ball close to the flag. Visualize the best way to play it and select the club that best helps you perform the shot. There's no better ally in these instances than experience. Constant practice and repetition on the course will help you learn to escape most problems successfully.

Chipping with a 7-iron from the fringe is an excellent stroke-saver. Stand with your weight on the left leg and hands ahead of the ball (top left). Swing the club back with little leg movement or wrist break (top right). The through-stroke is a pendulum motion (bottom right).

Becoming a sand-play artist

It's one of golf's oddities that sand, a course hazard designed to penalize a golfer for a wayward shot, does more harm to the poor player than the better golfer. Sand bunkers are more distressing for higher handicappers than low ones because they have such a rough time escaping from them in one shot. And even if they do get out on the first try, of the three possible results from a sand shot, two are bad. There's a good chance they'll have skulled the ball over the green or hit it fat and short of the putting surface. So whether it's a poor shot out of the bunker, or extra shots from it to get out, sand is the cause for many high scores.

Don't let bunkers penalize you more than they should. First, be positive about the shot. A positive attitude will eventually get you over the hump of being a bad sand player. If you continually believe that the next shot will turn the tide in being good in the sand, your skill will finally win out. When you begin hitting great shots from the bunker, it lifts your whole game a step and increases your overall confidence. A negative feeling will make your muscles tense and not allow you to swing freely. Second, think creatively about how to play a sand shot. Look at where you should land the ball so that it can get close to the hole. Visualize that shot and expect that shot. Imagine how hard to hit thc ball. Third, practice the shot using the proper technique so you build familiarity in your muscles.

Preparing for the shot

You can't hope to perform well out of the sand if you don't have a sand wedge in your bag. The sand wedge has the most loft of any club, and its sole is designed to cut underneath the ball. The club has a wide sole for more "bounce" than other wedges, meaning it won't dig into the sand. The softness of sand requires a club that doesn't go deep into it. The sand wedge's bounce helps the player cut a shallow area of sand from around the ball. You, in fact, aren't supposed to have the clubface contact the ball. The clubhead cuts underneath the ball, throwing out sand and ball together. If you hit the ball first, you'll likely hit it over the green. The amount of sand you hit, combined with your length of swing and swing speed determine how far the ball will travel. Over time, you will learn how to combine these three elements for the shot distance you face.

The usual sand shot will be from a greenside bunker, with the ball setting up on the top of the sand. The distance to the green can be anywhere from a couple of yards to 20 to 30. After you've examined where you want the ball to land, step into the bunker from behind the ball. Pick an aiming spot and step to the side of the ball. The Rules of Golf allow you to wiggle your feet into the sand for the purpose of getting a solid stance. You cannot attempt to further test the sand for how hard or soft it is. Position your feet in an open stance, and play the ball off the inside of the left foot. The wiggling you did lowered you an inch or so below the sand, so there is nothing else you need to do to have the clubhead cut underneath the sand surface. Your knees should be slightly flexed as always.

Lean left so that 80 percent of your weight is on the left leg. Aim the clubface at the target you picked out. As you stand over the ball, it will appear that the club is aimed way right—an open position—but that's because you have your feet opened up. Be sure to set the clubface open before taking your grip, not the other way around, which would "close" the clubface prior to impact. And the rules also say that since a bunker is a hazard, you cannot ground your club prior to the shot, so don't let the clubhead touch the sand.

Be still over the shot and quiet with the legs. Swing mostly with your arms. Take the club along your stance line going back, swinging it away from you. Hinge your wrists as you would normally. On the downswing, focus on having the clubface enter the sand an inch behind the ball, about the spot where you would have had the club hovering at address. Swing the club through with good tempo. Picture the clubhead shaving a shallow, dollar-bill size area of sand with the ball where George Washington's face would be. The ball should fly out with medium height. If struck well, it will land on the green and take a couple of hops before stopping.

Keep in mind a few truisms. First, the ball will leave the sand at about the same angle that the club entered it. When you swing the club with a sharp, V-angled swing, the ball will fly higher than a shallow, bowl-shaped swing. Second, the closer you are to the hole and the higher the ball needs to fly, the more you should open the clubface and increase loft. When you open the clubface, you take a more shallow cut of sand. Third, for long bunker shots, square

The sand shot: An open clubface and stance are part of the address position (top photos). The club is swung back like a sit shot moving out and away from the body and then across the target line on the downswing.

the clubface so the ball flies lower and travels farther. The less sand that is displaced and the greater the swing force, the farther the ball will travel. Fourth, the faster you swing your arms, the farther the ball will go, even if you haven't taken a longer swing. And fifth, remember that your goal is to get out of the sand, so don't expect professional results. Aim toward the flag if you can, but if there's no room, play to a spot away from the hole so you at least get the ball out. Oh yes, and please be sure to rake the bunker when you are done.

Variations on the sand shot

All sand shots won't be as "easy" as one from a greenside bunker. There are long bunker shots and fairway bunkers shots, as well as wet and hard sand and buried lies. Here's a quick look at how to play these variations.

Out of *wet and/or hard sand*, the idea is to play the shot more like a fairway pitch shot. The sand won't "give" as much as regular sand, so the sand wedge won't slide under the ball as easily. It would be like hitting a shot off of firm ice cream. The shot doesn't require as much force as normal. Don't displace as much sand. Position the ball toward the middle of your stance with a square clubface. Hit as close as possible to the ball with a sharply descending blow.

A *buried lie* is often referred to as a "fried egg." The ball is somewhat or fully covered in the bunker because the sand is fluffy or deep. You still want to get the clubface under the ball, but this is probably the only sand shot where you want to dig the club into the sand. Put 60 percent of your weight on the left side and have the ball in the middle of your stance. Play the shot with a square clubface. If the ball is very deep, close the clubface, meaning have the toe closer to the target than the heel. Swing up and down sharply, holding the club firmly. The clubhead will bury in the sand, stunting your follow-through. Hit into the sand as deeply as you need to get below the ball. You won't have much control over the ball, so just get it out. The ball will roll a long way, so only take as big a backswing as you think will get the ball to land on the fringe and then roll to the hole.

For *long bunker shots* of 30 or 40 yards, play the shot like one from wet and firm sand. Put the ball in the middle of your stance and square the clubface. Don't be cautious about taking a good cut at the ball. Swing a little harder than from a greenside bunker. For bunker shots around 40 to 50 yards, use your regular pitching wedge and swing fully, but try to intentionally take a little extra sand so that it cuts down on ball distance.

At times you'll find yourself in a *flat bunker with no lip* that leads right onto a flat grassy area before the green. The grass is regular or firm. In that case you should consider using the Texas wedge, your putter. Line up the shot like a putt, take your putting stance and grip, and punch the ball sharply so it scurries through the sand and grass and onto the green, where it can roll the rest of the way to the hole like a putt.

Learning how to play a shot from a *fairway bunker* can save you a ton of shots. Fairway bunkers are put around the area where drives land or come to rest. If you go in one, it's a wasted shot having to pitch sideways to the fairway. If you can learn to advance the ball a goodly distance down the fairway, you better your chance of saving par or getting no worse than bogey. This is probably the only bunker shot where you want to avoid hitting any sand. Definitely be sure to hit the ball first. If the ball is buried or up against the lip, use the sand wedge to hit back to the fairway. If the ball is sitting well and you can hit a longer iron down the fairway, stand with stiffer legs than usual and only lightly wiggle your feet into the sand, turning your toes inward. Choke down slightly on the club so the

When the ball is on a downslope in the sand, the club must be swung up abruptly (top right). On the downswing, the club follows the slope of the ground at the bottom of the swing arc (bottom right).

For a ball on an upslope, stand at address (left) with your weight on the right. Make a regular sand-shot swing (center), but let the club follow the slope on the through-swing (right).

When the ball is buried in sand, play it farther back in the stance (left) with the hands ahead of the ball. Swing the club up abruptly (center) and down as sharply. The follow-through (left) may not be as full as usual.

bottom of the swing arc doesn't catch the sand. Play the ball to the left of center in your stance. Swing normally, limiting the amount of leg movement. Try to clip the ball off the sand. You won't get your usual length, so hit one more club than you normally would for that distance.

Sand, hilly lies and you

The key for sand shots from *sloped bunkers* is to swing the club along the contour of the sand/slope. Otherwise your swing balance won't be correct.

For an *uphill lie*, put your body perpendicular to the angle of the slope, don't lean into the hill like it might seem natural to do. Your right foot and right shoulder will be much lower than their left counterparts. Play the ball forward in your stance opposite your left foot. Then make your regular swing, swinging the club along the slope. Let the club hit into the sand just before the ball. It should fly out with plenty of height. For a *downhill lie*, you still swing with the slope, but you must avoid hitting the back of the sand with the club. This time in your perpendicular stance, the left foot and shoulder are lower than the right of each. Play the ball off the right foot. You'll have to swing the club sharply up and down. Avoid hitting the sand going back, and make sure you go down after the ball so you don't top it on the downswing. Get a little wristy if you have to. The ball will fly lower and roll more than usual.

When playing a *ball below your feet*, your concern is making sure you stay with the ball. To set up, grip the club as close to the grip end as possible, and bend more from the waist. Position everything else as you would for a regular greenside bunker shot, except aim slightly left since the ball will likely go right. As you swing, your motion will be more upright than usual. Try to return the club back to its address position and don't lift your body until after impact. Keep your upper body steady.

More sand oddities

It's hard to imagine a ball staying *above your feet* in a bunker, but it could happen in soft sand. Choke down on the club, right up to the shaft if needed, and keep your arms extended. Aim to the right, how much depending on how high the ball is. Play the ball in the back of your stance and open the clubface. Keep your hands ahead of the clubhead on the downswing.

Once or twice a year you'll probably have an approach shot *plug into a bunker* just under the front lip. The recovery shot will test your strength. Stand as you would for an uphill bunker shot. Open the clubface. Swing the club into the ball so that it hits just underneath it. The club will bury in the sand, and the ball will fly out without spin and roll a far distance. This is one of golf's uncontrollable shots, so don't expect much. Be happy to get the ball on the green.

Except for the most manicured golf course, there are usually a handful of areas around the course where the turf is *a mix of sand and grass*. When your ball lands there, you'll pause and wonder if you should play it like a sand shot or pitch shot. If the lie is good and the ball sitting up, use a pitching wedge or 9-iron. Play the ball off your right foot and put your weight on the left side. Make your normal swing, but be sure to strike the ball first before the turf. However, if the lie is lousy and the ball sitting down, use your sand wedge and play the ball as if it was a regular greenside bunker shot. Open the clubface and swing the club up and down quickly and sharply. Strike the ground about an inch behind the ball. Be aggressive with the shot, because when the club hits the ground, the impact will greatly reduce swing speed.

7 Putting: Making Everything You Can

What golf means to: Louise Suggs, LPGA Hall of Fame member. "The greatest single lesson to be learned from playing golf is that of controlling one's thinking and emotions—mental discipline—which is of prime importance in the business of getting along with oneself and with others. The player who sincerely desires to progress in golf eventually discovers that displays of anger and impatience, however satisfying to her feelings at the time, merely thwart her hopes for decent scores."

There's really no substitute for having a sound, fundamentally correct putting stroke. That's why putting qualifies as golf's great equalizer.

Good putting helps golfers in different ways. If you're a poor player from tee to green, making a bunch of putts can balance the two areas out and make you an average player. You won't have many good holes, but by holing a lot of putts you'll save yourself from numerous bad ones.

And if you're a good player who hits a lot of fairways and greens in regulation, then putting expertise will transform you into an outstanding player. You will hardly ever have a bad hole and sometimes you will have superb holes.

Poor putting, of course, has only one effect. No matter how good or bad a golfer you are, lousy putting absolutely ruins your enjoyment of the game, piles up big numbers, and sours you on trying to improve in any phase.

With all that's at stake in the name of good putting, you really owe it to yourself to spend as much time as possible on the practice putting green grooving a dependable stroke. Moreso than for the full swing, golf courses are an ideal spot for putting practice. Not every golf course has a practice range. But almost every course has a putting green or two near the clubhouse available for use. On those greens you can spend countless hours honing your stroke. And it doesn't necessarily have to be done on days that you're playing, either. Most courses don't have any rules against nonplayers using the green to practice putt. (There could be rules against chipping, however.)

Frequent putting practice gives you the faith and confidence in your stroke to make a lot of putts. Practice ingrains proper procedures so you don't have to worry about mechanics on the course. You can step up to the ball after deciding on a line and make a smooth stroke without overthinking. The course isn't the time to get mechanical. It's when you want to have a positive frame of mind. You'll be surprised how effective your putting can be when you combine a good stroke with confidence.

Develop a regular routine to your putting. As you approach the green, look over

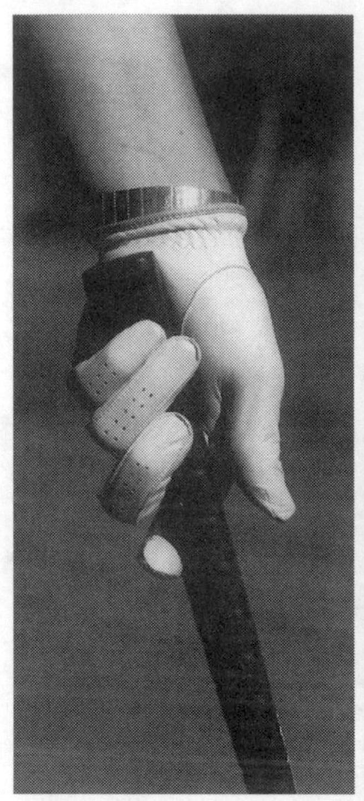
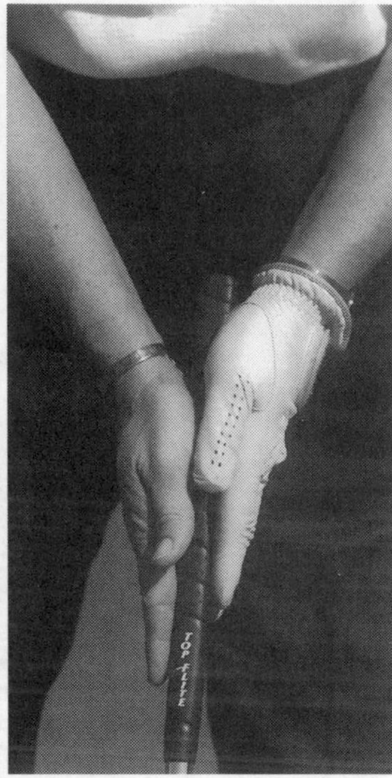
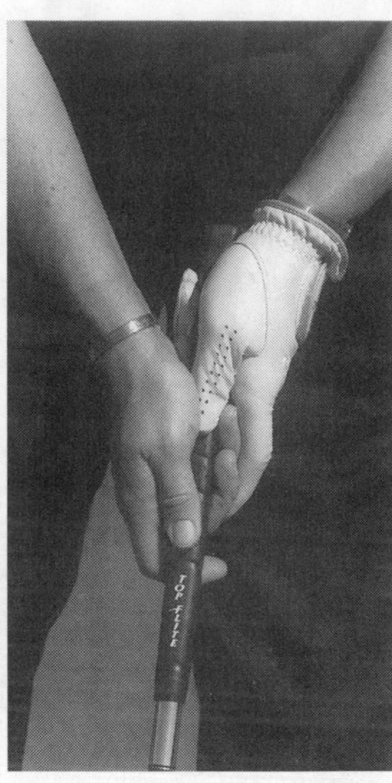

The putting grip has the grip running along the palm (left), as opposed to a full-swing grip in the fingers. The hands should be in an opposing position to putt (center). Both thumbs should sit on top of the shaft (right) once the fingers are wrapped around the grip.

the slopes that will affect your putt. Walk up to the ball, mark it and clean it. When it's your turn to putt, replace the ball, pick a line you want the ball to travel on, take two practice strokes standing to the side of the ball, then aim the clubface behind the ball and take your stance. Check the aim, look at the hole, check your aim again and then stroke the putt. The regularity of your routine will put you at ease. All that will be left for you to do is visualize making putt after putt.

Putt with feeling

As is the case with the short game, putting depends very much on feel and touch. That's why getting as much practice time as possible is important. Putting isn't like the full swing in which you're called upon to make aggressive movements with the entire body, hitting the ball in the air long distances. On the green you use a gentle stroke, standing still with most of your body while moving only your arms and shoulders. When struck by a putter (a club with a flat face), the ball rolls along the ground, rather than fly through the air as it does after being hit by an iron or wood. Being comfortable on the green has a lot to do with the kind of putter you use and how you stand over the ball.

Let's look at the putter first. It's about the length of a short iron, but it has a flat clubface so that when the club strikes the ball correctly, it causes a very slight hop before the ball settles to the ground and rolls end over end to the hole. (The hop is partially created because even though the putter looks flat, it does have around three to five degrees of loft.) There are an incredible amount of putter designs, much more variety than for irons. It's very important that you experiment with as many putters as possible. Never buy a putter until you try it out. Golf shop personnel will let you stroke a few putts with clubs from their display of putters. Discover which ones feel the best by trying them on the carpet in the golf shop or out on the putting green.

Some of the designs include the blade (a thin head that attaches to the shaft near the middle of the head), a mallet (half-circle in shape, looks like a flat metal wood), a flange (similar to a blade, but with an extension coming out from the sole), and a heel-toe weighted model (that looks like a cavity back iron and has a bent-neck hosel). Some putters have a hash mark or other directional marking on the top of the clubhead to help you find the sweet spot on the putter and align the ball with your target line.

That marking, or any aiming aid, is a feature you should have in the putter you purchase. You also want a putter that, when it is centered under your eyes, the sole rests flat on the ground so neither the toe nor heel are elevated. Get a putter with a grip that's flat on one side so your thumbs can lay flat. And a putter that feels heavy in the head will help you have better feel for the clubhead during the stroke.

Grip putter in the palms of hands

You may recall that your grip for full-swing shots is held in the fingers. The putting grip is mainly in the palms. To grip the putter, put the putter handle diagonally across the left palm to the base of the index finger. Close your hand and make sure the thumb sits on top of the grip. Your right hand goes on so that the thumb pad of the right hand sits on top of the left thumb. Check, too, that the right thumb sits on top of the shaft, the right little finger is snug against the middle finger on the left hand, and the index finger on the left hand sits on top of the fingers of the right hand. Hold the putter without tension. Feel at ease and comfortable, not rigid.

This grip helps you swing the putter back and forth with a pendulum motion of the arms and shoulders while the rest of your body, especially the head, remains motionless. The hands are in "opposition" to each other and should be positioned directly below your stomach. Bend from the hips to position your eyes directly over the ball. You can check this eye position in two ways. First, while crouched over, drop a ball from your eye level and watch where it lands. Or, let a putter dangle straight down from eye level. The point at which the ball drops or the shaft points is where the ball should be below your eyes.

The back of the left hand should face down the line of the putt. Have your feet no more than shoulder-width apart, square to the target line, and flex your knees so they feel springy. Your weight should be evenly balanced on both legs. In this posture, you should be able to turn your head only to the left and look down the putting line.

Stand over a putt with your eyes directly over the ball and your feet on a parallel line with the putting line.

Find the sweet spot on the putterface by dangling the club and striking the face with your finger. You've found the sweet spot when the face rebounds without twisting.

Using a range ball with stripes is a great way to learn how to line up the clubface with your aiming point.

Ball position also needs your close attention. As you make practice strokes, determine where the bottom of the swing arc is and keep it in sight because that's where you want the ball positioned. This spot will most likely be between the left foot and the middle of the stance.

Your alignment needs to be extra precise on the green since the slightest off-line set-up will make the ball miss the hole even if you make a good stroke. The alignment procedure starts by putting the putterhead down behind the ball first and checking that the clubface is lined up the way you want it. The idea is to first pick out the path you want the ball to roll on, then align the putter to that path. Next, line up your feet and body parallel with the intended path of the ball and in proper relation to the ball. As you stand over the ball checking that your putter and body are aligned correctly, focus on the distance of the putt and how firm you'll have to hit the ball to make it go that distance. Picture in your mind's eye the ball rolling on the line you've picked out to the hole.

Now you're prepared to take the putter back. Bring it back smoothly, remaining still. You don't have to be overactive with your body. Focus on moving the triangle formed by your shoulders and arms back and forth. Maintain a slight pressure in the left hand and keep both wrists firm, particularly the left wrist. The right hand serves as more of a guiding support. Maintain the angles formed by the elbows at address all during the stroke so that the swing arc doesn't shallow out or get more upright. Your right elbow should be tucked close to the body.

Don't let the putter slow down until the last moment of the through-stroke. Keep it moving from start to finish. It's not a quick-back-and-slow-through type of motion. You should try to make the backswing and through-swing about the same length, although it would be better to have the putter go more forward than backward. When you make a big backswing, the tendency is to decelerate the putter going forward. Thus, the huge swing you've made going back doesn't deliver much of a pop.

All of this good technique will be for naught if you don't strike the ball on the putter's sweet spot. This is the area on the clubface that hits the ball with the most solid

The putting stroke is a pendulum-type motion. The arms and hands form a triangle with the shoulders. Swing the triangle back and forth, maintaining its shape throughout. Keep the putter low to the ground.

feel because it either has the greatest amount of clubhead weight behind it, or, in the case of a heel-toe balanced putter, it is the balance point. The directional mark on the top of the putter usually indicates the sweet spot. To check for the sweet spot on your putter, hold it up high in front of you with two fingers of your left hand so that the putter dangles with the clubface turned toward you. Use your right index finger to strike the clubface in a number of spots. If the putter twists when you hit it, keep tapping until the clubhead rebounds without turning. That's the sweet spot, the most solid part of the clubface. Mark the spot on the top of the clubhead so you can use it as reference while practicing.

The art of green reading

The putting line you think the ball will travel on is determined after you have "read" the break of the putt. A putt will either have no break at all, or it will break left or right. Sometimes a putt may do all three, such as roll straight for a distance, break left and then break right. A putt can also go uphill or downhill, and have break at the same time.

As you face the hole, if the green is flat, which doesn't occur very often, the ball will roll straight to the cup. If the green is sloped from right (the high side) to left (low side), the ball will break left. If the slope goes left to right, the break is to the right. The amount of curve depends on the severity of the slope. Of course, if the slope is going away from you, then the putt will be faster than normal. If the slope is going upward and into you, then the putt will be slower. Hit the putt softer or firmer accordingly. Be aware that the softer you hit a putt, the more it will break. You need to allow for more break on a downhill breaking putt because you have to hit it softer. So think of speed when judging the break, then when you're standing over the ball, focus on distance and how hard to stroke the putt.

To read the green properly, you need to use your sight, hearing and touch. And you do need to be a good green reader because a good putting stroke is of no use if you don't know which way the ball will go. When you look at a green, see how tall the grass is (the taller the grass, the slower the putt). When you walk on the green, determine how soft or firm it is (a hard green means it will be fast). While walking you can sense whether you are going uphill or downhill. If your shoes make a crunchy noise as you walk, it's an indication of a fast, dry, hard green.

While you're walking to the green is another good time to read the lay of the land. Study the shape of the green and major slopes. These slopes might not be so visible while you stand on the green, particularly on a hillside. Here are some other tips to read greens:

1. You're better off reading too much break than not enough. Play the ball to the high side more than the low.

2. It is better to miss putts long than short. When you miss a putt long, watch how the ball goes past the hole. You can pick up a tip on how the short putt coming back will break.

3. Putts late in the day usually break less and are slower than those earlier in the day since the grass has grown.

4. On windy days, putts roll faster and break more since the grass dries out.

5. Observe the grass around the edge of the cup, or look closely at the green itself. You can often tell which way the grass is growing. When the grass is growing away from you, the "grain" will make the putt faster and curve it more than if the grain was into you. If the grain is growing to one side or the other, it will make the ball curve more to that side.

By recognizing how the slopes in the green curve the ball, you can combine your feel for judging distance and how hard to hit the ball with knowing the amount of break to play to be a putting whiz.

8 Unique Swing Conditions

Advice to first-time players: Kathy Whitworth, LPGA Hall of Fame member. "For women beginning golf, I stress the fundamentals. It's a mistake simply to pick up a club and start swinging. Take lessons from a competent professional—it's worth the money! Don't be in a hurry to get onto the golf course. The more time you spend on the practice tee or at a driving range, the better your actual style of play will be. Get your swing down before going out on the course."

Rest assured that the full swing you learned in Chapter 5 is, in fact, the only swing you'll need to enjoy this great game. It's the same swing that every golfer learns, whether that person is a woman, man, junior, senior, left-hander or from Antarctica. Everyone has the same fundamental swing to learn.

But, there is a "but" to that statement. Women will find that there are unique swing conditions that almost exclusively affect them. Some of them are caused by their comparative lack of strength. Some are just general things that women do that men don't. It's just the way things are, and it's important to recognize these specific problems so they can be effectively handled, thus relieving the woman player of as much frustration as possible.

It's a fact that men have benefited from a different sports environment than women. Men have played games all their lives, the same way it was for their fathers and grandfathers. Men have, for the most part, competed athletically all their lives. Most women have had to play catch-up, a difficult chore because for many years women were not a part of a systematic physical training program. But in recent years, girls have participated in sports in greater numbers. They are involved in organized sports, such as softball and soccer leagues. They've learned the motion of swinging a bat at a ball, thereby learning how to release power. These fine girl athletes, when they take up golf, are able to use their athletic skills and abilities to great effectiveness. In the past, good girl athletes might have felt they needed to hide their athleticism, but not so today. Such talent is much more appreciated.

As we well know, women are very much into physical fitness today, including the playing of golf. But there's still the problem that women are not as strong as men and their competitive attitudes must be developed further. Nature ruled that men were born stronger than women. If a woman and man of similar size, weight and build got themselves in the best physical shape possible, the man would still be about 20 percent stronger.

The great LPGA Hall of Famer Mickey Wright wrote: "Someone once explained it to me this way. A human muscle is like a rope of fibers that contract. A women's muscle is a comparatively little rope and a man's muscle is a bigger rope with stronger contractual power. To compensate for this lack of strength, a woman golfer should have no wasted motion in her swing so she can utilize all those voluntary muscles to their maximum efficiency."

Women and men have also had attitudinal differences toward why they play. Men mostly golf because they simply want to play. They feel good about themselves and feel they should play well. But they're impatient. They want quick results. It's tough for them to set realistic goals, partly because they overestimate how well they play. As Kathy Whitworth wrote: "A man is expected to pick up a club and break 90 before he's spent 20 hours on the course. A woman is not expected to be so adept, since she is usually considered helpless, unable to hit the ball. Fortunately, that's no longer true. Women have proved they can do just about anything men can. They certainly can play golf as well as men, but they are doing it in their own way."

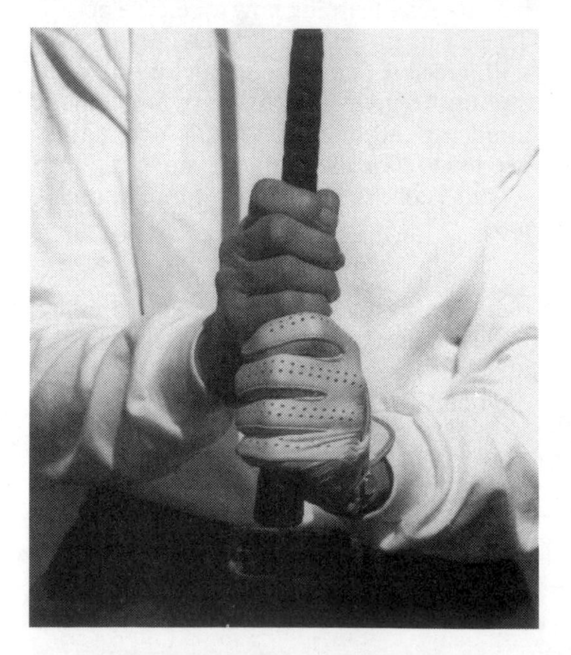

Using a 10-finger grip may relax the golfer, increase confidence and make her feel stronger.

Many women play because they want to join their friends and husbands, but they are made to feel bad about their golf and told they need to improve. Women are more willing to set up short-term goals because they don't overestimate their ability. Socially, however, women who practiced felt they might lose friends because although it's great to accept instruction, it wasn't great to take it to the point of practicing.

Today's woman golfer is not intimidated, though. If she wants to practice, there's nothing to stop her. And speaking of practice, it's always a good idea to get hooked up with a qualified teacher. You'll find a teaching professional at most golf courses and practice ranges. Check with your friends for someone they'd recommend. When you contact a teacher, ask about credentials and whether he or she takes new players. Discern whether you will be compatible with the teacher. When you get started, talk with him or her about what you expect out of the relationship, and your hopes and ambitions for improvement.

The following swing concerns don't affect all women, but you might find one that pertains to you. Included are thoughts on how to counteract the swing problem.

Coordinating the lower and upper body

Since men grew up playing a lot of baseball or softball, they have an easier time of feeling how their lower bodies should move during the golf swing. There's a similarity between the lower body movement while swinging a bat and that of swinging a golf club. Many girls aren't exposed to that chance, so when they play golf they have nothing to go on in learning how to move the hips and legs. It makes learning the swing that much harder.

Making long, relaxed swings with two irons is not only a strength builder, it is a good way to warm up by stretching muscles.

It's not that feasible to get a woman back out on the baseball field, so a good way to see how the upper and lower body must work together is to stand before a full-length mirror and make swings at an imaginary ball. The woman can see how the lower body moves through the shot ahead of the upper body.

While checking the lower body, keep good knee flex and have 70 percent of your weight focused on the balls of the feet, not toward the heels, another common problem among women.

Release elbow and shoulder tension

Some women have a natural tendency to push the club rather than swing it. They guide the club with the upper body rather than swing with a relaxed motion and let the big muscles of the body move freely. Tension builds up in the elbows and shoulders in particular. Thus the club is swung with stiff arms. This tension could be the result of feeling like the club has to lift the ball in the air. To counteract this thought, don't think of the club lifting the ball, but the ball getting airborne due to the clubface trapping the ball against the turf and the ball rolling up the face and flying up. The club strikes the ball just before bottoming out and then takes a divot, the small cut of grass and dirt.

10-finger grip relaxes arms, shoulders

It is best to use either the overlapping or interlocking grips described in Chapter 5, but there's a chance a woman will feel stiff and rigid in the arms and shoulders using either one at first. Until she becomes comfortable with her swing, she might be better off using the 10-finger grip. This grip increases confidence and makes the player feel stronger.

A long waggle helps start the backswing

Short, abrupt waggles prior to the backswing can make it difficult to swing the club back smoothly. Making a longer, stiff-wristed waggle gets a woman's forearms moving to start the backswing. Waggle the

For beginning golfers, clearing a water hazard is one of their main concerns. A good strategy is to never try to go over water unless you have a club you hit consistently well.

club until the hands are around waist high. This builds the sensation of the arms, shoulders and club moving backward together.

Tips on aiming

Not being target-oriented is a problem for some women when they address the ball, as well as during the swing. It's a mistake to walk up to the ball, plant your feet first in a comfortable position, then put the clubhead down behind the ball. Chances are you'll put yourself in a closed position, with the left foot much too close to the ball. You can't expect to get proper alignment that way. You can only do with the upper part of your body what your feet put you in position to do. A high percentage of shots are missed before the club is drawn back because women set up improperly. When the feet are closed, women block the upper body and can't make the club go in a true arc.

Instead, remember the procedure for getting lined up in Chapter 5. Stand behind the ball and pick out a spot in line with the ball and target that you want the ball to travel over. The spot could be a leaf or divot in line with the flag. Then go to the side of the ball, step up to it and place the right foot in position, then align the clubhead behind the ball. Let the vertical lines on the clubface line up with the aiming spot. Next, after lining up the clubface with the target, move the left foot into position and make an adjustment to the right, if needed. There still might be some feet adjustments to make, but the clubface should remain lined up to the target. This is the procedure to follow for all clubs.

The top of the backswing is another danger area for bad target alignment. Many women "lay off" the club at the top, which means pointing the club to the left of the target at the top of the swing. This causes a tendency to throw the club too soon on the downswing rather than letting the body turn bring the club to the ball. Look where your club is aimed at the top of the swing. If it's not pointing at the target—where you want the ball to go—adjust the club so it is. Form a mental image in your mind and make practice swings, trying to point the club in the right direction, which would put the club on a line parallel to the target.

Use idle time to gain strength

Because most women don't have strong wrists and forearms, they can't swing the club very quickly. Gaining strength is one of the few ways to increase swing speed and thus hit the ball farther. Swinging a weighted club is a tried and true method to increasing strength, but it's not always convenient to obtain a heavy club or find an area to swing one. A simple exercise is to take a club while watching television and waggle the club while sitting down. This builds strength to keep the club firmly in position during the backswing rather than wobbling.

How not to flip out

When women use equipment that's too heavy for them, they have to overwork their arms and shoulders. A bad swing fault resulting from this is spinning the upper body at the start of the downswing. The club swings down from an outside-to-in swing path. It may not only be the equipment that causes this, but most women feel that to get the ball up in the air they have to scoop the club, getting the leading edge of the club under the ball so it flips the ball up. This flipping effect is most likely to occur when playing chip and pitch shots. The ball doesn't get airborne due to a scooping motion, but instead by the loft of the clubface doing its part as the ball is struck properly.

Scooping the ball is what happens when the player overcontrols the club handle. To avoid this, think in terms of swinging the club with the forearms, not controlling the clubhead with the hands.

Lengthen arc for distance

You've learned that the average woman has less power than the average male. She can't hope to generate distance by making a short, compact swing. But since women are blessed with great mobility and suppleness in their joints and muscles, they need to take advantage of that and swing the club with as great an arc as possible. While making this big arc, hold on to the club firmly so you don't lose control at the top, and maintain a reasonably straight left arm so the arc remains big and the arm and shoulder muscles can stretch.

A good drill to make a full swing arc but avoid overswinging is to take the club by the clubhead and swing the club upside down, focusing on the handle. Extend the radius of your swing and make a wide arc, but don't take the club so far back that it begins to point toward the ground. Practicing this way gives you the triple benefit of more clubhead speed, more power and more control.

Be careful about what you feel might be a full backswing. You don't want to lose your swing connectedness. Some women greatly turn their hips and legs, believing it's a correct motion. Their hips turn as much as the shoulders and the legs are completely turned to the right at the top of the swing. If the club droops down toward the ground, you've gone too far. You certainly do want to make a full shoulder turn, but don't get overactive with the lower body. Keep your feet planted and don't turn your hips more than 45 degrees.

Adjust for full-figure "problem"

Women blessed with a full figure find that a large chest can get in the way of freely moving their arms. Some discover that by positioning the arms so that the right arm is to the side and under the right breast and the left is on top of the left breast, they can swing their arms without interference. However, this can cause the player to lift the left arm out of sync with the rest of the upper body. Most LPGA Tour players let their arms hang naturally to the sides of their breasts. When they turn their chest, arms, bust and shoulders in the proper motion, the problem of a large bust is lessened. In this situation, experimenting to find the best match of proper swing motion with comfort is the best way to go.

Clubhead speed provides distance

Some manufacturers use women advisors when they design women's clubs, but they are often strong players. Equipment companies that do more detailed research and development on the woman player produce clubs that are more in tune with the typical female player who isn't as strong. Most women need lighter clubs than the woman professional so that they retain control of the club better. Look to see if going to a lighter set of clubs helps you swing with more control. And lighter clubs will let you swing with more clubhead speed, which in turn adds distance to your shots.

Give the ball a solid hit

It's an unnatural movement for most women to release an object physically in a sport. Women have been taught to be so docile that the idea of accelerating the club and releasing energy is foreign. There is no swift-moving action into the ball, just a floppy one. Mickey Wright commented: "Apart from a woman's comparative lack of strength, I think too many women golfers possess an even greater weakness on the golf course. Women don't hit the ball as hard as they can. Too many don't hit the ball hard enough to leave the imprint of their swing on the turf, let alone know when or why they should take a divot."

Many women are afraid to take a divot, and are worried that they won't look graceful if they swing hard. So instead they swing with a loopy motion that doesn't deliver much pop. Sam Snead is said to have had a graceful swing, yet he delivered a strong hit to the ball. You can be graceful and swing hard at the same time.

Don't be indecisive

Course strategy is a gray area for many women. They need a guideline on how to attack the course, make a decision, pick a club and play the shot. How you plot your way around the course will improve the more you play. But there are some things you must know in order to play the round with as little wasted strokes as possible.

First, become familiar with how far you hit each club, especially the driver. By knowing driving distance, you can decide where to hit the ball off the tee, plus avoid trouble if you need to hit something less than a driver.

Second, always know where the trouble spots are on the course and play away from them. Don't take chances unless you're using a club you feel comfortable with and the result of a mis-hit won't put you in worse trouble.

Third, try to place your shots around the course so that you'll have a flat lie if at all possible. There's no sense laying up on a hole with a long iron if it puts you on a downslope. Use the middle iron and have a flat lie.

Fourth, on most bunker shots the goal is to get out on the first try. Don't risk a tricky shot if it might mean another shot from the sand.

Fifth, play away from wooded areas on dogleg holes. You may have a longer second shot, but you won't be in tree trouble due to a wayward drive.

Sixth, if a long par 3 calls for you to hit a wood, and you lack confidence with it, back off and play an iron to a spot short of the green, and hope for a chip and putt to save par.

Seventh, handle water hazards by playing short if you can't use a club you have confidence with to clear it. Perhaps you could use a 3-wood to clear the water, but it's not your favorite club. You're better off laying back in this instance and hitting your next shot with a club you're more successful with.

There are other strategy methods you'll learn as you go along. Just remember to play shots that keep you free from trouble. Only be daring when the odds are better than 50-50 in your favor.

9 Hints Especially for Women

Keeping golf and life in perspective: Laura Davies, international star. "I'm a golfer, not an exhibitionist. Some people accuse me of being underwhelmed by it all, but that's the way I am. It's not in my nature to jump up and down when I'm successful, and I'm never going to change. I'll have the same friends and be the same person. I'll enjoy the money, but I'm not so keen on making speeches or being on television."

Protocal. It's so important to know all of the nuances in golf to act properly, dress correctly, and fit in with your fellow golfers. In Chapter 8, you learned about specific swing problems for most women. Here we are continuing to focus on special areas that affect women only, including selecting the appropriate apparel, special physical concerns, such as playing while pregnant and handling osteoporosis, and advice on mixing business with golf.

Clothing: What to wear

Women golfers have had to overcome the stigma of being more fashion-conscious than player-conscious. Women were the ones expected to look good rather than play well. Dressed in pastel colors, with matching golf bag and hand bag, many women looked more appropriately dressed for an Easter parade than a battle with the golf course.

In the 1940s and '50s, short-sleeved shirts were acceptable. Women wore skirts. Then in the late '50s, country clubs allowed women to wear knee-length shorts. Flamboyant colors were in for men, which they had ignored before for the whites and grays they'd see Ben Hogan wear. One of the early concessions to making clothes more comfortable to play in came about through Babe Zaharias. She signed a contract with the Serbin clothing company. With Serbin, she helped design a women's golf dress that had pleated sleeves and an elastic waistband, with a large pocket for tees, balls, a scorecard and marker. The dress proved very flexible for swinging the club.

That convinced other clothing companies to jump into creative mode, thinking of better designs for useful, comfortable golf clothes that also looked good, wore nicely, were bright and durable. That continues to drive apparel makers today. Men have improved their looks on the course, while women have brought up their competitiveness to match their wardrobe. They haven't lessened their desire to look good, but they've softened on the look of solid, bright colors with the need to have crossover clothing to accommodate their active lifestyles.

You may be confused about what clothes are appropriate for the course. Obviously, public golf courses allow you to be looser

Dressing conservatively is the best way to go, but someone in the golf shop can help select an appropriate ensemble.

in what you wear. Your choice can range from a nice outfit to jeans and tennis shoes. But whether you are at a public or private course, you're better off dressing conservatively, mainly because that matches the way the game is. Golf has a lot of tradition, so anything too outlandish doesn't work well.

You can usually find out what you can and can't wear by checking with the golf course. Most of them have dress codes. What is usually not acceptable are cut-off shorts, short shorts, denim and lycra material, tank and halter tops, nongolf shoes, tennis clothes and jogging outfits and warmups. What is usually quite safe are slacks, knee-length shorts, skirts that drop 18 to 20 inches from the waist, and golf shirts, sweaters and vests. A quality pair of lightweight, sturdy spiked golf shoes rounds out a nice outfit. (Although the new spikeless shoes have won over many converts.)

Pregnancy and golf

Around 15 to 20 years ago it became more clear to doctors and women that there really was no reason why a woman having a healthy and problem-free pregnancy could not play golf well into carrying her child, even to the seventh and eighth month. In fact, playing pregnant could pay dividends, especially during the second trimester when morning sickness may not be as strong. Some women, because they have additional bulk, find they hit the ball farther. Others hit the ball straighter and more controlled since they can't move around as much. Their body remains steady.

Doctors have noted that swinging and walking are better as exercise than running or aerobics, which can limit the blood supply to the baby. During pregnancy, a woman's blood volume rises by around one third the usual amount. It's important that the exercise a pregnant women gets does not make her go beyond her target heart rate.

Women will discover that their address and posture positions change as the pregnancy continues. The back and abdominal muscles are stressed and the shoulders become more slouched with a heavier chest and stomach. The center of gravity continually moves and the woman has to adjust accordingly to get into a comfortable position. These adjustments include bending more from the waist, opening the stance more (moving the left foot away from the target line), swinging the club more outside on the backswing, and doing whatever else she can to feel comfortable.

A good rule of thumb to follow when pregnant is to simply not do any exercise that you can't perform while speaking in a conversational tone of voice, such as golf. If you're uncertain about your condition, discuss your hopes to continue playing golf with your doctor.

Here are some other tips and observations:

- Don't play during the last four to six weeks of the pregnancy since the baby is growing quickly at this point and you don't want to do anything to impede its progress. Plus you're at a time when premature labor could begin.

- As the abdomen gets larger, you'll have a particularly tough time putting and chipping. The grip sticks in clothing as you swing. A good way to get around this, literally, is to widen your stance and lower your body to the ground. This clears a path for the club and maintains a steady position over the ball.

- Avoid going out in hot and humid weather and in temperatures more than 90 degrees.

- If you are going to walk, use a pull cart so you don't have to bend over as much as you would with a carry bag. See if players in your group would be kind enough to take your ball out of the cup on each green.

- As you would normally in a pregnancy, eat well and snack on fruit. Avoid fatty foods since they make it tougher to lose extra weight after delivery. Drink plenty of fluids, and include foods in your diet that have carbohydrates and potassium.

- Be rested to start the round, and definitely warm up and stretch ahead of time. Take the usual precautions in sun and heat. Elevate your feet afterward.

- A good waiting time to come back after giving birth is around six to eight weeks, depending on how well the delivery went. If you're nursing, you may need longer time and will have to coordinate a nursing schedule with your golf activities.

- Be patient when coming back from pregnancy. If you had played up to your seventh month, you can feel comfortable that you won't have lost too much of your touch and ability. Do the normal exercises prescribed for women after giving birth. With the proper strengthening and exercise program, you will likely come back a better player. Many women feel physically stronger, emotionally stable, confident, and have an I-can-do-anything attitude following their pregnancy.

The effects of osteoporosis

This disease, which mainly affects women, causes weakening of the bones as people get older and the bone's mineral content leaches out. Thus it is a "silent" disease since it quietly does its damage. The bones become more fragile and brittle. It's a main cause of hip fractures in the elderly, and spinal compression fractures that result in a "dowager's hump." It may cause wrist fractures, which are difficult to treat because the bones heal so slowly and there's an increased risk of arthritis.

Osteoporosis primarily affects white, post-menopausal women, thin people, smokers, and people who drink alcohol to excess and use caffeinated drinks a lot. Certain antiseizure medications cause this as well. It will affect, with symptoms of some kind, nearly half of all women in their lifetime.

You can't change things if you are a woman and white and aging, but you can make some lifestyle changes to decrease the risk of getting osteoporosis. Cutting out cigarettes, alcohol and caffeine will help, as would taking calcium and Vitamin D supplements. All women—and men—older than 40 should supplement their diets with 1,000 to 1,500 milligrams of calcium and 400 units of Vitamin D per day. Once a woman has passed menopause, many doctors recommend estrogen supplements to slow down the loss of bone mass. There are some risks with this, so consult with an MD or gynecologist. The risks may be counteracted by taking another hormone, progesterone, with the estrogen supplement.

Osteoporosis shouldn't prevent you from playing golf or doing moderate exercise such as aerobics or easy weight lifting. You should be cautious of swinging too aggressively, however. But it's helpful to have the gentle exercise you can get from golf and walking to prevent bone loss.

Mixing business with pleasure

Men have been combining the forces of golf and business for decades, having known for a long time how compatible the two are. Golf and business only clash when you talk about the honesty and integrity of golf in comparison with some of the questionable business tactics used today. But the two work well together because of golf's ability to bring people together, who have practically nothing in common, in a social setting. Once two sides have been brought together on the golf course, there is a great chance they can agree upon a piece of business that is mutually helpful.

In recent years, women have cashed in on this partnership that was once the man's domain. The male golfer used to be easily defined as a working man who played golf for fun at times and for business other times. The female player was someone unemployed and usually the wife of a club member or a male golfer. Now women golfers are also busy career women climbing the corporate ladder.

The problem is, most career women have been unable to enjoy the same golf course privileges that "the old boys" of the business world have. At private clubs, women's playing times have been limited and the problem compounded by ladies' day taking place during the work week. Scheduling a time to play casually or with a client, plus practicing, has been as difficult as closing a business deal. Women are forced to play in the evening, trying to network with clients without the benefits they know a golf environment can provide them, and must play corporate golf without chances to practice.

There are some courses that have changed their tee-time policies to make it more open-ended and conducive for everyone. But some business women have grouped to ease this problem even more. The result is the phenomenon in recent years of several golf leagues or associations for the business woman or executive. These leagues, some with their own home course, emphasize the usual areas you'd see at a club, such as posting scores for handicaps, playing a variety of courses and holding clinics and tournaments. They have regular meetings to schedule outings and golf trips. Basically, they give the woman player all the social ramifications golf can provide and that the male player has been getting all these years.

Two organizations that have gone national in order to create chapters in cities around the country are the Executive Women's Golf League and the Professional Businesswomen's Golf Network. Not only have they tried to bring businesswomen together for social golf and to build a business network among them, but they have promoted interest in the game with junior girls and catered to new players.

PBGN director Patt Fero considers their work to branch out into other cities a steady and growing effort, and says the difficulty

Golf shop personnel are being trained better than ever to understand the needs of the woman golfer. If they fail to do so, they are losing out on an important segment of the market.

lies in retaining women who start off in the program with strong enthusiasm, but slowly lose interest. In that sense, Fero says rules and etiquette clinics to make women feel comfortable are high priorities. "We found, too, that it's helpful to have beginners stay together and have experienced players mentor them," she says, to help newcomers learn how to act socially as golfers.

PBGN can be contacted at P.O. Box 25518, Greenville, SC 29616, phone 803-895-6377. The EWGL, which recently aligned itself with International Management Group, the sports marketing and management firm, has 75 chapters and more than 5,000 members. To contact the EWGL, write to 1401 Forum Way, Suite 100, West Palm Beach, FL 33401, or phone 407-471-1477.

Although most women don't play golf for its potential to help them in business (more than 50 percent of females play for golf's recreational, social and fitness aspects, only 8 percent for business), business golf has gotten a lot of attention in the women's world and the population of businesswomen is growing. It has been projected that by the year 2000, about 50 percent of all new players will be women. And since women are more and more being put in managerial positions, women, business and golf will be more connected than ever. Thankfully, golf's handicapping system can put business clients on the same level with everyone else. You may not be equals in the business world, but on the golf course everyone is on equal footing.

Businesswomen like golf for the same reason men do. When you're put in an administrative position, there is a strong need to accommodate clients and entertain them. A round of golf is great for that purpose. You can make connections, and network out with business relationships. You can find out about their personality, how they do business and how they interract with people, since most people conduct their business affairs in the same manner that they play golf. Business golf is the forum by which you can build a closer relationship with a contact than just talking over the phone. And once you make contacts, things begin to snowball. New contacts continue to be made.

More and more women today are taking part in corporate outings, where various heads of state from different companies meet on the golf course to socialize, talk business and play golf. Most women who haven't been a part of this scene will likely be nervous and concerned. The important thing to remember, however, is that many men are in a similar boat, and that these outings are important events in the business world. The men you play with may play only a few times a year and be equally uncomfortable. The key is to go into these outings with a positive attitude, enjoy them and have fun, and realize that there will likely be players doing worse than you. It helps if you ask ahead of time what format will be played so you can study how things will proceed. Be honest and up front about your abilities. Don't oversell how good or bad you are. Ignore as best you can any ill treatment by men who might resent your presence or be upset that you're beating them. Their attitudes are deep-rooted and you won't change them in one afternoon.

In Chapter 4, you learned the basic approach to arranging a golf match and how to act on the course. If you're playing with a business client at a public course, those procedures still hold up. But in business golf at a private club, you have to be doubly sure everything is covered. How the day goes will very likely affect how the rest of your business relationship continues.

You could play just as a twosome with your client, but that person might feel more comfortable if you had a neutral party or another client. However, if you have more people from your company than clients, there might be a feeling of being surrounded.

Be sure to call the club ahead of time to check whether you do or don't need a starting time, and make sure there isn't an event scheduled for the day you've picked. Recheck the club's policy on when men and women can play. A woman joining a club for business reasons will probably not have elected to be at a club that has restrictive times, but if you are, make sure everything works out so you aren't embarrassed.

Tell your guest what the dress code is, not only for golf but for dinner if you'll stay at the club. Don't take things for granted. Some clubs don't allow spiked shoes any more and only allow the newer spikeless kind. Provide the guest with accurate directions. Clearly establish a meeting time and tell him or her where you both will meet at the course. Check on whether a locker will be available so the person can drop off any personal items right from the start. Look into whether your guest likes to walk or ride, and then plan accordingly. Don't force a rider to walk or vice-versa.

Punctuality and dependability are very important in your golf outing. Arrive at the course on time and don't make your guest wait. Time is as important to them as it is to you in the business world. Upon arrival make sure you're registered in the golf shop and settle any costs. As host, you're responsible for all fees. Find out when you can head out to the first tee. Have enough small bills on hand to tip the support staff when needed, such as the locker-room attendant, shoeshine person, cart boys and bag handlers, and caddies (the professional staff usually does not get tipped). Usually a couple of dollars for each person is fine. Caddies could be tipped an extra $5 to $10, but check with the caddie master. There may be a rule against tipping beyond the regular fee.

It's always a good idea to have some extra money in case there's a wager on the line. You may not need to have something to play for (and thank goodness for that), but so many business people feel they have to play for something. The most common money

A business-golf outing or golf date should not be a tense situation. They are set up so the business associates can enjoy their golf and each other's company first of all and establish a business contact second. Of course, that contact will become more important later on, but it's the golf game that has brought the two sides together.

game you can play is a $2 to $5 nassau. Betting anything more than $5 units is not necessary. In a nassau, you play match-play style for the agreed-upon amount. There's a match for the first nine, second nine, and 18 holes as a whole. You can include handicap strokes, and you can agree to have a press bet, meaning that when one side is a certain number of holes down, such as two, there is an automatic doubling of the bet for that hole only.

There may be other kind of "junk" you agree to play. One might be greenies (hitting the green in one on a par 3 and making par or better), sandies (saving par from a greenside sand bunker), barkies (hitting a tree and still making par), an Arnie (making par without ever being on the fairway), a Watson (chipping in for any score), longest drive, fewest putts, and so on. These side bets could be worth the same money unit as the nassau or less. A good golf dictionary or betting book (such as Golfgames, by Rich Ussak, Contemporary Books) will make all betting terms clear to you.

Don't make excuses about how you're playing. No one likes it when someone constantly moans about the lousy day they're having. If you're a good player, but aren't doing well, your playing partner will recognize how well you swing. You'll hit enough good shots that he or she will see your talent. All golfers can sympathize with someone having troubles since all golfers have a bad time of it every so often. So maintain an upbeat attitude and avoid being a whiner.

Remember that how you treat the course and its personnel tells a lot about how you would treat business people. It shows attention to detail that will not go unnoticed. Also be aware of how your language might be taken and control your anger. Vulgar language and attempts to be like "everyone else" are inappropriate. Be on your guard to act professionally. You're with a client, not quite a family member. You want to be casual with the person, but not frivolous. Lastly, play by the Rules of Golf. Know them well so you can be sure to add penalties when needed. If you aren't aware of the correct way to handle a situation and forget to add strokes, it might be taken as cheating.

When the match is done, offer to have a drink, lunch or dinner. Exchange business cards if needed and remind the client why you were wanting to get together in the first place. Then tell him or her that you'll be giving them a follow-up call in the near future. Avoid talking too much about a business deal on the course.

Guarding against harmful rays

Everyone should be aware of the danger of too much exposure to the sun's ultraviolet light. But because sunlight can cause a serious illness like skin cancer, persistent aging and browning of the skin, or eye problems, it's worth including helpful tips in this chapter.

Tans are caused by the sun's ultraviolet A light, and burns are the result of the stronger ultraviolet B light. So the goal is to block out the B light as much as possible so the A light can still tan without burning.

Sunscreens and lip balms are the most common approach to preventing burns. And the best sunscreen for you to purchase is the kind with the chemical PABA (para-aminobenzoic acid) listed as an ingredient. Applied properly, PABA creams accumulate under the skin and provide protection even after a swim or shower. PABA creams still allow some A light through to let you tan. Experiment with finding the right cream that doesn't cause you to have slippery hands or irritate your skin (which alcohol-based screens can do). Make sure the cream you get has a standardized sun protection factor (SPF) of 15 or more. As an option to cream, zinc oxide completely covers the skin. However, some people find it unattractive, although it is made these days in colors such as blue, white and green.

Protection against the harmful effects of the sun takes on many forms. A special umbrella (right) designed to keep the user cool while the sun blazes away has helped many golfers avoid heat stress. Material has been developed for shirts (below) that blocks out the sun's rays quite effectively, at a rating of around 30 SPF.

The type of clothing you wear can also block harmful light. White cotton, for instance, along with other light-colored clothes are somewhat effective, but like most material, they become useless when soaked with perspiration. That's why it's even a good idea to not only put sunscreen on your face, arms and neck but also on your upper body before dressing. Recent developments in clothing, however, have resulted in material that can effectively shut out the sun's rays. One example is Solumbra, with an SPF of 30-plus, developed by Sun Precautions and able to block out 97 percent of the harmful light.

And as more incentive to play well, you'll find that you decrease exposure to the sun's rays by keeping the ball in the fairway. Grass only reflects about 2 percent of the sun's rays during the noon hour. Sand bunkers, however, reflect 20 percent and water hazards about 10.

Ultraviolet light can create eye problems, such as sties, iritis, pinguecula and pterygia. The latter two are related problems of a growth on the white of the eye. The growth can become large enough to affect the cornea or pupil and blur vision. It's also possible that UV light will create cataracts or even cause macular degeneration, which affects the retina and may bring blindness.

Hats shade the sun from directly hitting your eyes, but wearing sunglasses while playing is becoming a more popular trend. Golfers may have resisted sunglasses in the past because they made it hard to read greens. But today's fashions are lighter, smaller, better looking and more effective in cutting out UV rays. It will probably take you a couple of months to get used to a pair, but it would be worth trying. The best color lens is brown, pink, vermilion and gray, in that order; the worst are green, blue, yellow and orange. And be sure the lens has been coated with a UV shield.

Another way to avoid harmful light is to schedule your golf game in the early morning or late evening so that you miss the most damaging time period of 10 a.m. to 2 p.m. And don't be fooled by a cloudy, summer day. The sun's UV rays can still penetrate the clouds.

Staying in shape

Probably the best way for you to get in the kind of physical condition you need to play good golf is to play the game as much as possible. The more you play the more you'll build endurance. Walking an 18-hole round while carrying your bag probably burns 600 to 700 calories.

Since your legs need to be in good condition to walk the golf course, try some kind of aerobic exercise, such as jogging, stair stepping, walking, bicycling or jump rope. These activities improve your leg strength, and also exercise the lungs and heart for a general feeling of physical conditioning. Taking an aerobics class is of equal help.

Be sure to maintain or build flexibility. Your shoulders and back are very important in this respect, but also critical are flexible hip joints. Use a stretching program on a daily basis or see a physical trainer.

Golfers don't need to build muscle bulk, but they do benefit from being strong in certain areas. The hands, wrists and forearms should be toned to help grip the club and prevent injury. As mentioned, the legs need to be strong to walk the course and propel the downswing. And a strong, supple back is needed to stand up to the rigors of swinging for an entire round and practice sessions.

Change equipment in later years

Senior women experience a decrease in strength, and muscles become less flexible. To help fight these natural bodily changes, an equipment alteration is in order. Clubs with graphite shafts, although more expensive, are lighter and will be easier to maneuver. Look into other equipment changes that can make the club lighter.

10 Solving Shot Problems

What golf means to: Sandra Haynie, former LPGA star. "Golf is a natural course for women. There is no sport that I can think of that offers so much satisfaction, so much enjoyment and so many benefits to women as golf does. Not only are you able to get out in the fresh air, but you also enjoy nature. Of course, every day won't end with a beautiful sky and every drive won't be down the middle, but it will still be rewarding fun."

The more you learn about the swing, the clearer it becomes that things aren't going to be a walk in the park on the golf course. You're going to hit a lot of wayward shots that put you in difficult positions to recover from. Playing these recovery shots with a degree of expertise will go a long way to cutting down your score. There are times when you have to hit a low shot, high shot, curved shot, even a lefthanded shot, to advance the ball down the fairway or put yourself on the green as an escape around trees or another obstacle.

All of these shots don't mean you need to relearn a basic swing. But they do mean you have to understand ball flight, have good visualization skills, and be willing to practice different techniques to make the ball react in certain ways. It helps, too, to understand the differences in hitting a short iron and long iron, which is what we'll discuss first.

Differences within the set

You've learned that there are some alterations you have to make during address when swinging a short iron compared to a wood. Here are some basic rules when you switch from a long club to a short one.

As clubs get shorter, your stance gets narrower, your hands and the ball get closer to your body, and you bend more from the hips. Your swing also gets more upright, but the backswing shortens. The ball is positioned off your left heel, but it will be closer to the middle of your stance since the stance has narrowed. Your swing with a shorter club will be more straight back and up, rather than more around and flatter with a long club. And for a shorter club, the swing arc is more pointed at the bottom and the club comes down steeply to the ball. With longer clubs, the bottom of the swing is a sweeping motion.

When you practice with each club, observe where the bottom of the swing arc falls so you can position the ball at those spots. When you're setting up to play an iron for a tee shot, always put the ball on a tee so the ball rests just atop the turf, giving yourself a perfect lie.

As the club gets shorter, your stance narrows by bringing the right foot closer to the left.

You might feel you have to make a swing adjustment with a long iron, but the swing stays the same. Don't make the mistake of altering posture and address. Keep your feet about shoulder-width apart, weight balanced, hands level with the ball, and position the ball a little left of center. Resist trying to scoop the ball up with these long clubs. Swing normally and trust the loft of the club to lift the ball.

When hitting woods, golfers have a sense of power, just the opposite of the long iron. There is a lot of mass with a wooden clubhead and thus substantial confidence. Because of this, it's important not to get carried away and feel like you need to smash the ball with a wood. Save your hardest hit for when you want extra distance. Swing the woods with control and tempo so they can work effectively.

With your irons, you learned to swing down on the ball. When playing a wood, the swing path should be level to slightly ascending. The shaft length of a wood makes you stand more upright than an iron. Play the ball off your left heel. When you practice with the driver, try to keep the tee in the ground after impact, which will indicate that you've swept the ball rather than hit down. When teeing the ball for a driver shot, set the height so the equator of the ball is level with the top of the clubface. Hit the ball on an ascending path. Don't try to be too precise with this club. Aim for the biggest area of the fairway. The bigger the target area, the less pressure you'll feel. For distance, the two keys are clubhead speed and contact. The ball won't go very far without both. Make sure all parts of the swing work in order, and that nothing is outracing anything else, such as your arms overtaking the lower body.

For fairway wood shots on a tee, tee the ball so the top of it is level with the top of the clubface. Don't hit down on a teed ball with a fairway wood since the ball will sky too much. You do want to hit downward, though, with a 3-wood or lofted wood when the ball is directly on the turf.

For a partial shot, swing the club forward to match how far it was swung backward.

Hitting partial shots

Not every shot has to be hit with full force. Wind, soil conditions, and the design of the hole, by themselves or in combination, may force you to make a swing change. In that case you'll probably have to play a partial shot.

You use the partial shot when playing to hard greens and there's room to let the ball roll to the hole. Rather than fly the ball to the hole, a partial shot can land short of the green and roll to it. A partial shot is also good into the wind since it makes the ball fly lower. Make sure you use extra club, however, in whichever situation you use the partial shot because there is a loss of distance. So, the partial shot rolls more, goes less distance, and flies lower than normal.

Any club can be used for a partial shot. Whatever length you swing the club back, you swing it a similar amount forward. So you could swing your hands back until they are waist high on the backswing and forward swing, or shoulder height back and forth. It's like making a full swing, except the backswing and through-swing are shorter. Don't decelerate the club coming down, and make sure you transfer your weight as you would normally. Plan this shot with some creativity and execute it with feel and motion.

Getting out of trouble

Every golfer knows the feeling of being trapped. You've hit a wild shot and now have to recover from some off-the-track part of the course. For most beginners, it's best to just hit the ball back onto the fairway, using a lofted wedge if you're in high rough, or a low-lofted club if under a tree. Get yourself back into play and go on from there.

If you have faith in your ability, then be more daring to escape trouble spots, send the ball further down the fairway, and in the end keep your scores from going out of whack. You must feel confident in your knowledge about the swing, you need to have your swing under control, and you have to be creative in visualizing how to play out

The partial shot above shows the hands being swung around shoulder height. Notice that the weight is still transferred from one side to the other. Compare the length of swing to a normal shot (below).

of trouble. Picture how you want the ball to fly out of a bad situation, and think of how you need to alter your swing to make the ball fly in the correct manner, low or high, curve right or left, and so on.

Don't confuse making a safe effort at escaping trouble with a miracle shot. For all of the trouble shots described later, don't proceed with an escape shot unless you have more confidence than doubt that you can pull it off. Pick your spots. If you're at a point in the round where a rash judgment would cause you more problems than a safe shot, don't be heroic. The idea is to get out in the fewest number of shots, not in the most spectacular fashion. Allow yourself some margin for error. Don't play a shot too close to trouble so that if you mis-hit the ball you can still be in good shape.

Your ability to maneuver the ball and create escape shots may very well be the final step in becoming a good player rather than staying a poor or average one. Shaping your shots and making the ball fly the way you want it to opens up a whole new style of play and puts you in control of where you want the ball to end up. Golf becomes less of a guessing game.

Avoiding trouble in the trees

To hit a *high shot* over trees or to clear an obstacle in front of the green, position the ball more forward in your stance than normal toward the left foot. Set your weight more toward the right side. This tactic adds loft to the club, moves the bottom of your swing arc and helps you make a higher finish. Use one more club than normal for the shot since you've added loft. Play the ball about an inch closer to your body. The ball might go left to right, so aim a little left of the target. Swing the club with a sweeping motion, but don't lift.

To hit a *low shot* under trees or to run the ball onto the green, position the ball toward the back of your stance, no farther forward than the middle. With this change, make sure the clubface is still square to the target line, otherwise you'll hook the ball. Have more of your weight on the left side, which moves your hands ahead of the ball, off your left leg. Grip down an inch on the club and stand about an inch closer to the ball. Make a normal swing and focus on solid contact. Swing easier and shorter than usual. Keep your hands going through impact ahead of the clubhead. Strike the ball first before the ground, pinching the ball. Keep your hands low at the finish. Since you've taken loft off the club, the ball will fly lower. You may need to go down one club since the ball will roll more.

Many golfers may not need to learn how to *hit a slice* since it's their normal ball flight. But for players needing to intentionally curve a ball from left to right, align your body—shoulders, hips, knees and feet—left of the target and aim the clubface at the target. The clubface is in an "open" position and will cut across the ball for a clockwise spin. Normally you line up the clubface and then your body. For this shot, line up your body first before you aim the club. Use your normal grip, but position the ball more forward than usual. Swing the club along your feet/stance line. You'll feel the club swing away from you on the backswing, and across your body on the through-swing. Use your left hand to pull the club down and through so the right hand doesn't try to turn the clubface over. The ball will start along your stance line and then curve right. The ball will probably start higher than normal, so go up a club from what you would normally use for the distance.

To *hit a hook* or ball with right to left curve, align your body to the right of the target, but aim the clubface at the target (making it "closed" to the target). Position the ball to the back of your stance, how much depending on how much you need the ball to hook. Place your weight more to the right. Make your regular swing, but swing along your stance line. The club will swing inside toward you, and then continue out away on the through-swing. The more the ball hooks,

For uneven lies (top photos), position the body so the spine is perpendicular to the ground. Then swing the club along the slant of the slope. When the ball is in rough (bottom), try to catch the ball first and avoid having grass get trapped between the clubface and ball.

the lower it will fly. Allow enough room on the left for the ball to roll after it lands; because of the extra roll, use one club less than normal for the distance.

Playing in *windy conditions* is one of golf's mysteries. Into the wind the ball flies higher, comes down sooner and rolls less than normal. With the wind, the ball goes lower, remains in the air longer and has more roll. The wind can turn a ball left or right, hold it up or knock it down. Not only is the ball affected, but the player is likely to be thrown off balance. When it's windy, focus on swinging with good tempo. Don't try to overpower the wind. Stand wider, swing with control and make good contact to lessen the wind's effect. Play the ball back in your stance to hit it lower, shorten your swing for more control and use more club if needed to overcome a loss of power. When putting, stand a little wider and crouch more. Stabilize yourself, but don't change your putting stroke. Make solid contact and accelerate the putter through. Unfortunately, you can't do much about how wind affects a putt that's rolling. That aspect is out of your hands.

You can tell *wind direction* by looking at the flag blowing on the flagstick, studying the tops of trees, tossing grass in the air, observing how other players' shots react, and looking at water. Water looks choppy when the wind is blowing downwind, but it seems calm upwind. When the wind is crossing, it turns the ball and brings it down sharply, often causing a sideways bounce. Determine how this will occur and, if you can shape your shots, try to counteract the wind. Make the ball fly left to right, for instance, and work it into the hole if the wind is blowing from right to left. If you have to hit a straight shot, and the wind is going right to left, for instance, play the ball well to the right depending on wind speed and let the wind blow it back to the green.

Hitting the ball off of *hardpan* is a nervy feeling because there's a fear of hitting the ball thin or bouncing the club off the dirt into the ball. Hardpan is that bare-dirt lie you might see where people have walked a lot or where carts have been constantly driven. You could consider putting the ball from this lie if it's around the fringe. Otherwise, to just get the ball back in play, use a pitching wedge and narrow your stance. Pull the left foot back off the target line to open the stance. Position the ball off your right foot and put your weight on the left side. Grip the club a little lighter than normal. Swing with the thought of returning the clubface back to its position at address. Keep the left arm moving, making sure to keep the hands ahead of the clubhead on the through-swing. Hit with a downward movement. If you need to advance the ball down the hole, use a middle iron and play the ball back in your stance. Grip down on the club. As you swing, take the club back and up sharply and come down and trap/pinch the ball with the clubface.

Don't get wristy or flippy with the club

Playing from *deep rough* leaves you two options. If you luck out, you'll have a good lie and can play a middle or long iron or wood. If you're unlucky, your only choice is to use a lofted wedge to get out of trouble. To play a longer club, be absolutely sure your ball is sitting well and that your club won't get tangled up in the high grass. Eliminate any tension you feel, be relaxed and position the ball in your stance as you normally would. Put more weight on your left side. Open the clubface slightly and aim to the right since you will probably pull the ball. Swing the club up and down more abruptly than normal. Swing aggressively and keep your left hand moving to prevent the club from catching. Swing to a high finish. For a lofted wedge shot, stand as you would for a greenside bunker shot, with stance open, weight on the left side and ball in the middle of the stance. Your head and hands should be on the target side of the ball. Cock the wrists early on the backswing, and swing the club out and up. Be firm with your grip and swing down more steeply than normal so that when you strike down behind the ball, there's less chance grass will grab the club.

When the ball is on a *severe upslope* and you have a short distance to the hole, it's hard to gauge how the ball flight will be affected. Put all of your weight on the right side and use your left side for a brace. Hit something more than you normally would for the distance from the hole because the slope adds loft to the club, going to a 9-iron instead of a pitching wedge, for example. Aim a little right of the flag since you'll probably pull the ball. And be careful how you ground the club; the ball will sit precariously in this position and could be moved if you press grass down behind it. Make your normal short-iron swing, returning the clubhead as it was at address. Keep your hands ahead of the clubhead and the left wrist firm. Let the club stick into the ground and allow the loft of the clubface to pop the ball up and away. The hill will deaden the club, so don't expect much of a follow-through.

It seems unfair to have to play from a *divot hole*, left by some golfer who didn't play with common courtesy. But there you are, with your ball in the hole and unable to do anything about it according to the rules. You could be upset, especially after a great drive, or you can get out of it as best you can. You do that by positioning the ball in the middle or just right of middle in your stance, have your hands slightly ahead of the ball and with the clubface square to the target. Swing the club more upright than normal so that you swing downward at the time of impact. Make a good shoulder turn and shift your weight coming through. Keep a firm grip with the left hand to keep the club moving. The ball will fly lower, so plan for it to roll more than normal after landing.

Because of the odd shapes seen today in putting greens, you can expect at some point to have to *putt the ball from one part of the green through the fringe to another section*. Rather than chip over the fringe—a shot that requires a great deal of skill—use your putter. Line up the break of the putt as you normally would, but play the ball back in your stance toward your right foot. Keep your hands ahead of the ball. The tricky part is to swing the putter up sharply and hit down on the top, back of the ball. The ball will pop up in the air and bounce through the fringe before settling down as a regular rolling putt on the other green section. Since the ball spent little time in actual contact with the fringe, it will not be sent off line as much. You'll have to practice this shot a lot to get the hang of it. You can also use this technique when you're putting a ball from within a few feet of the fringe.

Playing off hilly lies

Sidehill lies need not be a major balance problem if you take care of a few things at the address position. You need to allow for how the ball will curve and adjust your aim accordingly. When the ball is below the feet, it curves right; above the feet to the left; on an uphill lie to the left, and on a downhill lie to the right. To play a ball below your feet, for example, if you did everything as usual, you would be leaning over at address and the force of the swing would make you fall over. Square contact is very difficult. To play this shot, you have to be stable at address. Widen your stance and flex your knees to get down to the ball, don't just bend over from the waist. Place most of your weight on the heels. Positioned this way you'll see the ball is closer to you than normal. Grip as high on the club as possible. Take a few practice swings to get the feel for the bottom of the swing arc. Position the ball in that spot. Aim more to the left. Swing smoothly and keep your weight on the heels. Use one extra club to make up for a possible loss of distance. The set-up is reversed for a ball above the feet: legs are stiffer, back straighter, you're farther from the ball, gripped down on the club, aligned more to the right. Swing to a high finish rather than around your body so that the ball doesn't go too much from right to left.

For *uphill and downhill lies*, the key is to make sure your body is positioned perpendicular with the slope of the ground. An uphill shot is usually played blind, meaning you're playing up a hill and can't see where the ball will end up. Stand with your weight on the right side and have your shoulders parallel with the slope. Your left leg is a brace. Aim a little more to the right and hit a club with extra power for the distance you have so you counteract the tendency to pull the ball and adjust for the ball to fly higher because of the slope angle. Position the ball toward your left foot (which should be where the bottom of your swing arc is) and choke down slightly on the club. Swing smoothly so that the club follows the shape of the slope. Pull the left arm through with speed. For downhill shots, the task is even more difficult if you are long-iron distance from the hole because the slope delofts whatever you play, making a 9-iron more like an 8- or 7-iron. From downhill lies you usually have to hit back up to an elevated green or fairway. It's not recommended that you swing anything more than a 5-iron since only the best players can get a long iron in the air from a downhill lie. Switch the stance elements for this shot: ball back in the stance, weight on the left leg, aim left to allow for more curve to the right. Your shoulders should be parallel with the slope. Swing the club down the shape of the slope, and limit the use of your legs. Because loft is taken off the club, go down a club to allow for greater distance.

Hitting a *shot over water* causes all kinds of tension in the golfer's body. Muscles tighten and the player's thought pattern goes into red-alert mode. As with any trouble shot, the key is to eliminate the danger from your mind and focus on how to pull off a successful shot. Don't think about the water, think about your target, either the green or a portion of the fairway. If you're in a situation where you're trying to clear the water, not just laying up, go through your usual pre-shot routine of gauging distance and what club to hit. As you get ready to hit, think about a good swing thought that has been working that day and use it with good tempo. Swing with assurance, don't quit on the ball. Don't beat yourself down with negativism.

Playing a *shot left-handed* (or vice versa for a lefty) is a great stroke-saver when you can't play from your usual side. Done correctly, you can advance the ball quite well out of trouble. The best club to use is a 5- or 6-iron turned upside down. Clubs with too much loft cause you to scoop the ball. Play the ball in the middle of your stance and adapt to a new grip as best as you can. Hold the club comfortably, either with a full-fingered grip, the Vardon (overlap) or interlocking grip. Choke down on the grip to allow your arms to move freely. Make a putting-stroke type motion, with your hands going about waist high on the backswing and through-swing. Keep your body still and make sure you hit the ball first before the ground. A simple back-and-forth motion is sufficient to get the ball airborne and out of trouble.

The most productive short-game practice will be done when you use a place that has a large green with many flag locations and a few bunkers around it.

The Art of Practicing

What practice and concentration meant to: Babe Didrikson Zaharias, the late LPGA Hall of Fame member. "It's hard to keep your golf game in the groove if you aren't getting steady practice. And then there's the way too many distractions can reduce your effectiveness as a tournament player. I'm talking about the mental side of the game—the mental concentration you need for big-time competition. When I've been thinking about too many other things besides golf, and my mind isn't clear and easy out there, then I don't plan my shots the way I should. I don't see the one right place where the ball should go. I'm just keeping the ball in play."

How often have you heard "practice makes perfect"? It may not even have been in the context of learning golf or any other sport. Anytime you've learned something new, you've probably heard that phrase. There is a lot of truth to it, since you can't read the instructions on how to assemble a product or see something demonstrated and expect to perform the task well if you don't practice it over and over.

The first time through any new activity is always a struggle. We feel uncomfortable and ill at ease. It is only after constant rehearsal and repetition that we become comfortable. And once we feel relaxed, that's when real learning begins. We do the newfound skill with freedom and confidence, no longer worried that we are doing what the instructions told us. We understand what needs to be done and we do it with sureness.

Today's practice phrase has changed in emphasis. Now it is "perfect practice makes perfect." The thinking is that we should not just practice for the sake of practice, aimlessly repeating a drill without concern we are doing it correctly. Practicing something over and over with wrong technique is nearly as bad as no practice at all. You may feel you've increased muscle memory, but you've only ingrained the wrong method. Perfect practice makes perfect means practicing with proper method so you don't learn a skill full of faults.

Productive practice is necessary to become a good player. There's no way to avoid it if you want to achieve golfing success.

The best way to practice

A productive practice session, on days when you aren't going to play a round, should last about 45 minutes on the range, hitting about 100 balls with your woods and irons. That should be followed by 45 minutes of short-game work, then 30 more minutes on putting. If you play at a private club, it will undoubtedly have a good practice setup, with a full-scale range for hitting woods and irons, a short-game area around a prac-

To practice full shots, set up a few clubs so that they help with alignment. Always aim to a target.

tice green, and then one or two large practice putting greens.

If your club is not like that, or if you play golf at a public course without a practice area, you'll have to locate a driving range or an indoor practice facility in your area. At these ranges, large buckets (about 75 balls) will cost $4 or $5. Smaller buckets with 35 balls will run $2 to $3. The newer style of indoor practice ranges has a variety of options. You can hit shots off rubber mats, use a swing analyzer, practice short-game shots and putting, and as at a regular outdoor driving range, there is usually a teaching instructor or golf professional who can help you for a fee, often for a half-hour session.

Notice that this schedule is for a practice session, not as a warm-up for a round of golf. Such a practice would give you two hours of work, most of it on the "feel shots" of short game and putting. If you can't spend two hours, at least spend most of your time on the feel shots, except if you're having trouble with a club such as the driver and need to work out a problem.

Dedicate yourself to the practice session with an attitude of working hard and being serious. Don't overdo the workout, however. Remember, you want to stay fresh for your next session. Schedule your practices throughout the week. Don't just hold an eight-hour session one day and then not practice again for seven to 10 days. You'll develop good habits faster with frequent practices. Have a plan in mind at the range. Know what you want to work on, perhaps certain swing thoughts or a skill you just picked up. Don't hit balls absentmindedly. Make sure your fundamentals are correct, such as grip and stance, and always hit to a target. On the course you always aim toward something, either an area in the fairway or the flagstick or a portion of the green, so you should also aim at a target in practice.

Take your time with each ball. Don't rush the practice. Step back and go through your pre-shot alignment with each shot. When you're tired, don't force it. Swing easier with the long irons and woods when you're weary. Mix up the clubs you hit so you don't tire yourself out hitting 50 driver shots in a row. And don't get into prolonged practices when you're swinging well. You may think the more you practice while your swing is in the groove, the better off you'll be and the longer you'll stay that way. You risk the chance of being bored and stale.

Getting better through drills

One way you can make your practices be perfect is by using drills. While they are not as ideal as having an instructor by your side, drills accurately show you how a certain swing movement feels. The best drill is one that doesn't need a lot of set-up time. Some drills don't require a ball or club and are just as effective as if you were attached to some fancy contraption.

Here are some drills worth trying to see how effective they are for you. Experiment with all of them to see which ones work best, then add them as a permanent part of your practice.

Full-swing drills

1. Most players swing faster than they think they do, and faster than they really should. To find a good tempo, take your 7-iron and swing at what you think is half your normal speed. Hit balls at that speed, and work your way through your bag to the driver. You'll hit the ball more solid and still maintain good distance.

2. Similar to that drill is the three-speed drill, in which you tee up three balls in a perpendicular line to you about a foot apart. Use a 5-iron and swing at the first ball with about one-third your full power. Swing at two-thirds speed for the second and then full speed for the third. You should find that the two-thirds speed gave you your best result. Use that speed all the time for consistency and control, and you'll leave yourself extra power to hit the ball farther when you need it.

You can lengthen your swing and increase flexibility by taking a driver or pole and swinging back and through so that the club points at the ball at each extreme.

3. To swing with balance and learn timing, use any club in your bag, stand at address and start the backswing. Lift your left foot and at the same time point the left knee in the direction of the right knee. After swinging to the top, begin the downswing by placing the left foot down and lifting the right foot and pointing the right knee toward the left leg. Learn to do this without delay and you'll understand the swing motion better.

4. If you have a loose grip at the top of the swing, and thus "throw" the club for a slice or fat shot, do this to build constant

Improve short-game accuracy and feel for distance with these drills. Chip to a golf bag placed on its side (top photos), using a pair of clubs for direction. The same can be accomplished by sticking a shaft in the ground (below). For both drills, vary your distance from the target.

grip pressure: Place a penny between the base of the right thumb and left thumb within your grip. Make your swing and keep your hands together so the penny doesn't fall out.

5. Many golfers have a tendency to scoop their long irons. Remember that the club should be descending into the ball, not coming up. To learn this, try to hit the ball so you make a divot on the target side of the ball, beginning at where the ball was at address. Make several practice swings to find the low point of the swing arc where you make a divot, and then position the ball accordingly.

6. To start the swing with a low, smooth takeaway, put a tennis ball behind the clubhead at address. Take the club back, keeping the back of the clubhead and the tennis ball in close contact for as long as possible until the club goes up naturally. Your arms will swing back low and wide.

7. If you swing your woods aggressively but don't see good results, you must have faith that a more-controlled swing with less effort will produce longer shots. A good drill is to take your 3-wood and swing it at a speed you think will make the ball go the distance of your 7-iron. Practice this for a few sessions, then try to make the 3-wood go 5-iron distance. All parts of your body will work together. Continue this pattern until you're up to swinging the 3-wood nearly full speed.

8. To overcome a slice, picture that a three-foot high mud bank is between you and the target and only a few feet to the left of you at address. Swing the club with the thought that on the through-swing you will stick the toe of the club in the mud wall. Your shots should straighten out.

9. To learn to swing the arms together, practice swinging them apart. Tee up a ball, take your 7-iron, stand at address, then put the left arm behind your back. Make an easy swing with the right arm, simply making contact with the ball. You'll probably whiff the ball often to begin, but keep trying. Do the same thing with the left arm, putting the right behind the back. Then alternate shots with each arm alone, and complete the drill with swinging the arms together. Try this for 15 minutes each time you practice.

10. You can learn a proper weight shift by starting the swing from the finish position. Stand in the correct follow-through position and feel how your weight is on the left side. Swing back down to the address posture. Then make a swing with the idea in mind of getting back to the follow-through position.

Short-game drills

1. To practice different heights and trajectories of pitch shots, take a trash can or large barrel and prop it at different angles. Then at a distance of about 30 yards, try to hit shots that go into the container at a similar angle.

2. Improve your aim on short shots by putting your golf bag on the ground and angling it away from you. Stand about 20 yards away with any club from a 7-iron to pitching wedge, and try to strike the

If you're leaving your putts short, put a tee at the back of the cup and hit the ball so it strikes the tee before falling in.

bottom of the bag by hitting a group of balls. Once you start hitting the bag, make the target smaller by putting a shaft in the ground. If you need help getting lined up, put clubs on either side of the ball to get aligned.

3. Along with aim you need to have feel for chipping and pitching. At a practice green, put three to five objects, such as a head cover, at 10-yard increments. Using a variety of short-game clubs, pick out an object and hit a ball to that distance. Don't hit to the same object twice in a row. You'll learn how it feels and looks to hit these shots of varying distances.

Every breaking putt could really be considered a straight putt. When you decide how much break to play, imagine a tee marking a spot next to the hole. Then stroke the ball toward that spot. You can actually put a tee in the ground during practice.

Sand-shot drills

1. Most sand shots only require you to take a thin sliver of sand along with the ball, about a dollar-bill size. One way to learn that is to get into your address position for a greenside shot and draw a line about one to two inches behind the ball. Swing the club so the clubhead enters the sand at that hash mark.

2. Another way to take the right amount of sand is by making six-to seven-inch long by three-inch wide ovals in the sand and hitting the sand out of that area without a ball. Let the club go no more than a half-inch or so below the surface at its lowest point. Once you're comfortable with this, draw the oval and rest a ball in the middle of it, then swing again with the same intent in mind.

3. Lastly, another image of how thick or thin you want to slice the sand is to take the peeling off an apple or pear. As you stand in the bunker, use that image to visualize how deep the club should penetrate the sand.

Putting drills

1. To get a feel for distance, stand at one spot on the green and pick out three locations to putt to of varying length along the fringe. Then putt a ball to each spot, trying to get the ball to stop at the edge of the fringe.

2. If you have a problem with leaving putts short, put a tee at the back of a hole on the inner edge so the tee is at a 45-degree angle. Now putt the ball from short range so it hits the tee and falls in.

3. For help in picturing how break affects a putt, locate a putt on the practice green about 10 feet in length that has plenty of curve. Visualize how the putt breaks and put four more balls at two-foot increments along that break line. Then, beginning with the shortest putt, stroke each ball into the cup, allowing for the right

Hitting shots out of the bunker means taking a small oval or circle of sand around the ball. Practice this by drawing a circle in the sand. Either hit the sand circle without a ball, or place one at the back of the circle.

amount of break. If you've misread the break of the 10-foot putt, set yourself up again and rehit.

4. To get a feel for the greens at your home course and how they break, go to the course at times when it's vacant, such as the evening, and putt to tees you've stuck in the green at possible hole locations.

5. This game will keep you interested in learning to putt as a contest in improving long-range putting. Locate a putt of about 30 feet and putt 10 times to the hole. Give yourself two points for each putt made, one point for each putt that finishes beyond the hole but within three feet. After you've made at least 10 points in your 10 balls, go again from a greater distance.

6. To get a sense of what each arm does in the stroke, putt with just the left and right arms alone. Try this for about a five-foot putt. Avoid getting wristy with either arm. Bring the arms together at the end and see how they work as a unit.

7. To make sure you swing the putter on an inside-to-inside path, rather than outside the target line, put a board on the other side of the ball from you, positioning it about a half-inch away from the toe of the putterhead. Swing the putter back and through, not hitting the board. Use this drill on any length putt.

8. Another drill to get feel for putting different distances is to stick about 10 tees at about three-feet increments from one spot. Have a dozen balls or so at hand. Pick out a tee and putt the ball to that length. Pick out another and putt to that. Alternate tees and continue to get a feel for how hard to hit the ball different distances.

When attending a professional tour event, take advantage of the closeness to the players and learn from their technique.

9. The putting stroke should be balanced, meaning you swing the club past the ball the same distance you took the club back. To learn this, find a level putt on the green. Put three tees in the ground, on a parallel line, the first one where the ball would be, and the other two about five inches on either side of that tee. Then practice by putting a ball near the middle tee and taking the clubhead back and through to the tee markers.

10. To make sure you're striking the ball at the bottom of the swing arc, picture the grip end of the puttershaft pointing at the same spot on your body throughout the stroke. You can test this by taking another club and gripping it with the putter while standing over a ball. Extend the other club upward until it makes contact with your chest. Now swing the "club" back and forth, always maintaining contact with your body. Notice where the clubhead bottoms out. That's where you should position the ball. That point should be under the left side of the face, and/or opposite the inside of the left foot.

Other ways of learning

There are other ways to learn the swing in addition to taking a lesson, attending a golf school, practicing on your own with drills, and reading books and magazines. TV golf, clinics, and attending tournaments are other ways the astute golfer will observe mannerisms and technique that might work for her own game. Here's how.

Clinics are popular formats because they're brief but informative. They last about an hour and focus on one subject, such as the full swing or putting. They are usually outdoors at the practice range or putting green, with ample seating set up for observers. And they are headlined by someone with expert knowledge.

If you attend a clinic, arrive about 10 to 15 minutes prior to the start to get a good vantage spot. If this is a clinic in which you'll participate, go through a 30-minute warm-up period so you're set to be your most effective. Be a good listener and don't be afraid to ask questions. Be willing to do the things that are asked of you. Bring a notepad to take down important points, but don't try to do everything the instructor says. Work on one idea at a time; too many thoughts cause you to feel mechanical. Work on what's been told to you when it's practice time, because that's where the ideas you've learned will be ingrained into your swing, particularly an important change such as grip.

There is more *golf on television* than ever before, now that there is a cable channel exclusively for golf. Most of the time we watch golf on TV to find out the outcome of that week's pro tour event. But the sharp-eyed viewer can pick up tips that are worth copying. In particular, watch the players' tempo and pre-shot routine. Don't start playing like the slow pokes, however.

Look for the players that are your size and see what they do that you don't. See how players assess a shot situation. They look things over, check yardages and wind condition, talk with their caddie, visualize the shot, take their stance, waggle the club and swing. The good players can do this in a matter of seconds. Follow their example. Also notice their composure. It's easy to be relaxed when you play as well as a professional, but even when they hit a bad shot, most react with level heads. They keep their concentration in check to make a good recovery shot and not hit two bad shots in a row. Picture what you do when you hit a bad shot and learn how to act next time.

The slow-motion swing replays are particularly good to see how each part of the body works. If you can, use a full-length mirror to duplicate things the pros do that you feel you don't do. You'll see a lot of putting, too, in slow motion. Notice the various putting styles and see that no matter how different these great players look stroking the ball, they all accelerate the putter. They don't let the club slow down at impact. If they do, the commentators mention this because it usually occurs at a critical moment in the tournament when pressure forces a bad stroke.

At a *tournament site*, you can use these same methods to learn from better players, except for the slow-motion replay, of course. Get a pairing sheet for the day and select one of two viewing methods. Either pick out a favorite player to follow the entire round, being sure to get into good vantage spots around the tees and greens, or situate yourself at one central location that allows views of a couple of holes. Staying at a difficult par-3 hole or sitting at the 18th green are good spots.

Being a "part of the action" is a major responsibility. You should follow several tips to be courteous to players and other spectators. Following these tips will make sure you don't embarrass yourself and can enjoy the tournament.

Remain silent and motionless when a player is studying and hitting a shot. Whisper if you have to say something. Wear comfortable walking shoes and clothes. Don't bring a radio, TV or phone. Be aware of where you are on a hole and where the players are so you don't get struck by an errant ball. Remain behind the gallery ropes and only cross the fairways where indicated. Be alert, keep your head up and don't walk through bunkers or across greens and tees. And don't ask for autographs from a player until they've completed the day's round.

Take the time to warm up

Earlier you had learned about how to practice on days you weren't playing. On game days, however, you want to adjust your warm-up routine. If you were to practice for two hours before playing, you'd wipe yourself out and have little chance for a good day. That's why you need to approach your warm-up time with a different game plan. Practice is reserved for learning good technique and grooving your swing. Warm-up sessions are for getting prepared and loose for the day's round, finding a tempo that feels good, and mentally readying yourself for that first tee shot. Don't substitute a warm-up as a practice session.

It's recommended that you warm up for about 45 minutes before playing. Arrive at the course early enough to get signed in, change your shoes and clothes if needed, then proceed to the practice range. Do some light stretches to loosen the back, legs, shoulders and arms. Slowly swing a weighted club or two long irons together. Put a club across the middle of your back and swing your upper torso from side to side.

Begin the warm up by hitting short irons, swinging smoothly and with good tempo. Give yourself plush lies and make good contact. Build confidence early. Hit around five balls with each club, gradually moving up through the bag to your driver, skipping every other club. Go from your pitching wedge to 8-iron to 6-iron and so on. After hitting the driver, finish with a few more wedge shots. Proceed to the practice green and hit a few chip shots and putts. Get a feel for the speed of the greens. Most of the time you'll find that the speed of the practice green is similar to the greens on the course.

If time allows, play a "practice round" at the range. When you're done with your full-swing shots, picture the first hole in your mind and hit a driver shot. Then hit the club you normally would for the second shot. Continue until you get to the green. Then go through the same routine for the second hole and so forth. This helps you become target oriented for the day and mentally sets you for the first tee shot.

If there is no practice area at the course you're playing, you can still warm up. Arrive around 30 minutes before your tee time, stretch your muscles, and after finding a location out of harm's way, go through your bag and make practice swings with your clubs.

In whatever manner you warm up, remember that you're only trying to get warmed up, not burned out. Don't leave your No. 1 game on the practice tee. Get yourself to feeling comfortable and set realistic goals for how you want to play that day. Avoid rushing to the course, and blazing through a dozen putts. You'll likely miss each one and then go to the first tee doubting your putting stroke.

Golf's emotional side

Emotions can very well get in the way of your ability to perform to your best potential. They affect that important area of concentration and being focused on what you need to do. After learning the golf swing itself, concentration is probably the most important thing to being a successful player. Without a clear focus, bad thoughts enter the mind and affect the way muscles tighten up.

Concentration is the total involvement of your mind and body in fulfilling the task at hand. For golfers, that is the preparation to play, plan each shot, and then swing with control to hit the shot the way they visualized it. You must consider each shot as a new challenge. If you have a 7-iron shot, you'll undoubtedly have played a 7-iron many times before, but on that particular day in that particular situation, it's a new shot for you.

There is the chance that for you, golf is a way to escape and relax from an intense world. In that case, you may not feel the need to concentrate on your golf game. For those who want to score as low as possible, concentrating at golf means doing the same things they've been asked to do at work, at school, at home or wherever else they face having to do their best.

Ben Hogan was known for playing golf in near silence. That's how strong he concentrated on his game. JoAnne Carner, on the other hand, is a loose spirit who interacts with the gallery. Which style is best? There's no question that Hogan had little trouble concentrating on each shot. But Carner can shut out everything else when it comes time to play. Most teachers agree that to ask golfers to focus on golf for four to six hours straight is not necessary. The action in golf comes in short spurts as a player hits a shot, walks to the ball, and hits again. Golfers should take short mind breaks. Think of golf as needing around 60 seconds of your total focus up to about 120 times a round, depending on how many strokes you average. The rest of the round you can give yourself a mental break. Don't fret over the next shot because you don't know the lie of the ball or other shot conditions until you get to the ball.

Your concentration should begin at the practice tee as you warm up. Focus on what you want the ball to do as you hit each one. On the range, check the wind direction, condition of the turf, get used to looking at a target, and play each warm-up shot as a regular shot.

Having a regular pre-shot routine also helps you concentrate. It puts you in constant tempo each time you swing and gives you a mental checklist to run through to make sure you're ready to take the club back. Whenever you go through your routine, your body is prepared to respond. Visualize the shot you want to play, and after going through your routine, picture hitting a successful shot.

Don't let bad shots make you lose your focus. One poor result is a small percentage of your entire round. Keep trying your best on each shot so you can cut down on the number of poor swings you make. If you're a beginner, this is especially important. You'll make a lot of triple, quadruple and worse bogeys, so expect a period of struggle. But keep doing as best as you can. Keep the swing thoughts to a minimum.

During those times when you feel overwhelmed by your failures or by the pressure of the situation, take long, deep breaths. Bring the air in deep and release it slowly. This relaxes you, as will shaking your arms and leg muscles to get rid of tension.

Golf is obviously a game of ups and downs. The downs make you upset, while the ups will please you. When bad things happen, remember that the world will continue, you're trying your best, your friends will still love you, and that you'll have the challenge of playing golf again another day, and hopefully play it better. When either something good or bad happens, maintain your emotions at the same consistent level. It's at that level that you can do your best thinking and stay clear-headed to make your best swings.

The clubhouse: The place where golfers of all ages and backgrounds meet to rehash their rounds and develop friendships that can last a lifetime.

WHAT DOES THE FUTURE HOLD?

What golf means to: Mickey Wright, LPGA Hall of Fame member. "Something happened to me when I swung a golf club. I felt free and graceful. Golf to me is not only a way of life, it's a creative outlet; a constant, never-ending challenge; frustrating, but never dull; infuriating, but satisfying."

From Mary Queen of Scots to Babe Zaharias to Nancy Lopez to the next generation of female players, golf and women have seen quite an evolution and the process continues. The two haven't evolved at the same rate, however. As a game, golf hasn't always brought women along through the changes made in equipment, access to courses, development of the professional tours, and many of its other multifaceted areas.

Women have certainly had an understanding of where they stood in the sport for decades, but may have felt powerless to do anything about it. Many of their concerns today, inequality in particular, have roots that go way back. In this commentary by a woman, which appeared in an article in The New York Times, you get a feel for the frustration she felt about the subject of course access:

> *Although golf has been called a royal game, its privileges, in this country at any rate, do not appear to descend in the female line. The Salic law is applied to this ancient and honorable sport. In spite of the fact, or perhaps because of the fact, that thousands of women play golf at scores of clubs within a 50-mile radius of Times Square, certain restrictions have had to be thrown about their use of the courses. This may be one of the next points of attack for the ardent feminists, some of whom would doubtless insist that they and their sisters had quite as much right at all times on the links as the mere men. However, whatever suffrage the women members of the many clubs may have, it does not appear to have been exercised to extend to them the unlimited usage of the course.*

Sound like the feelings of a 1990s woman? Yes, but this was written in 1916, and nearly 80 years later women still feel that same frustration over equal privileges. Rare was the occasion, in years gone by, when someone was moved to action. The fine Canadian amateur, Ada Mackenzie, refused to put up with discrimination any more and created a women's only club, the Ladies' Golf Club, in Toronto in 1924. The

Women are gaining more respect for being intelligent and proficient teachers of the swing.

club still exists and it gives women all the privileges that men get at most clubs. It is the only club in North America that is owned and operated by women; nearly 10 such clubs exist in Great Britain.

In recent years, barriers have been breaking down as women have taken stands on what's important to them: challenging course restrictions at private clubs, seeking equal respect with men as people who love to compete and play the game, and looking to have a voice in the way the game is governed and led into the coming years.

The statistical story

What's going to happen for women golfers in the future? Statistics that analyze women and golf show a mixed bag. (All data is from research done by the National Golf Foundation, unless noted.) A general consensus is that women are taking up the game in strong numbers, but also leaving golf in similar fashion. The majority of women are attracted to golf because it means a chance to relax and socialize, but there is a feeling of intimidation, even for experienced players, that sours the overall experience.

The female golf population has fluctuated since 1988. There were 24.5 million golfers in 1993, 19.3 million males and 5.25 million women. Of the golfing population age 12 and over, 78.6 percent was male and 21.4 percent women. In 1988, there were 5.11 million women players, but there had been nearly 6.5 million in 1990. Numbers for male players show a similar rise and fall pattern, from 17.8 million to 21.3 million and down to 19.3. The end result is that women were 22.3 percent of the golfing population in 1988, but had dropped to 21.4 in 1993.

The percentage of women who are beginners has slacked off. In 1988, women were 41.8 percent of beginners; in 1993, it was down to 37.3. Even with the drop, that is still a higher percentage of women beginners than women as a part of the total golf population, the previously mentioned 21.4 percent. There have been big increases in female beginners in two age groups. Thirty to 39-year-old beginners have increased 18.2 percent from 1988 to1993, and beginners age 60 and above increased 84.3 percent in the same time period. That latter group only totals 29,300 women. The number of female beginners between ages 30 to 39 is 238,000, and between ages 18 to 29 it's 298,000.

Despite the influx of new players, there are a substantial amount leaving the game. Of the 5.4 million women playing in 1992, 1.2 million didn't play golf in 1993, an attrition rate of 22 percent.

Of experienced players, the average female golfer is almost 41 years old, has been playing for nearly 11 years, plays 18 rounds a year and has a household income of $54,700. That compares with men's figures of 38 years old, 15 years playing, 21 rounds and $52,900 income.

The average woman has increased the number of rounds she plays during the year. In 1993, women played an average of 18 rounds, an improvement upon a 14.0 average in 1990. However, compared with their percentage of the golfer population, women have dropped. In 1988, women were 22.3 percent of the golfing population and played 19.4 percent of the annual rounds. By 1993 the figures had dropped to 21.4 and 18.8, respectively.

Today's woman golfer is more affluent than 1988, when less than 35 percent of all female golfers were from households with incomes of $50,000 or more. By 1993 the figure was nearly 50 percent. Similarly, the average household income for women players increased to $54,700 in '93 from $45,400 in 1988.

The female golfing population has gotten younger. Almost 53 percent of all female golfers in 1993 were below age 40. Within that grouping, female players of ages 12 to 17 have increased from 3.7 to 6.2 percent since 1988. The participation rate has increased among 30 to 39-year-olds since 1988, up 41.3 percent. That's in the category of core golfers, those women age 18 and over who played eight or more rounds during the year. Many of these players are undoubtedly businesswomen picking up the game.

The two age segments that have increased rounds played most since 1988 are 12- to 17-year-olds (up 113.6 percent) and 30- to 39-year-olds (up 53.1 percent). However, the 50 and over crowd, made up of retirees and members of private clubs, still play the most rounds of any women's age group. Thirty to 39-year-olds average 9.5 rounds played compared to a 43.1 average for women 65 and older. Fifty to 59-year-olds average 28.1, and 60- to 64-year-olds are at 36.2.

Men are still, far and away, playing the most golf of either sex. In 1993 there were 498 million rounds played, 405 million by men, 94 million by women, a percentage comparison of 81.2 percent to 18.8.

Most women—74.6 percent—play their golf at public courses, indicating either an unwillingness or inability to get into a private club. The type of women playing would indicate they have the resources and wherewithal to play private golf. Nearly 44 percent of women golfers have careers in professional management or administration. Other career breakdowns include blue collar at 18.8, clerical/sales (17.9), retired/not employed (13.7) and other (6.2).

What's actually happening

Beyond the statistics, the actual events taking place all indicate positive advancements for women.

More women are being put in executive positions within the golf industry than ever before. Judy Bell became the first woman member of the U.S. Golf Association executive committee a few years ago, and could eventually be elected USGA presi-

More and more women are being hired in golf shops to serve the needs of both women and men customers.

dent. Equipment and apparel companies have placed women in management spots. Women teaching professionals continue to show their expertise, dozens of them being named head professional or director of golf. Each time a woman is put in a position of prestige, it allows them to be a part of the decision-making process.

Groups such as the Executive Women's Golf League have been popping up to give women a stronger position in getting access to golf courses, introducing golf to new players, and teaching them how to use golf as a successful business tool.

Programs for girls have shown steady improvement. The LPGA maintains two programs that assist girls with learning to play—the Inner City Junior Program and the Junior Girls Golf Club. The Inner City program started in Los Angeles for underprivileged kids and is now in Portland and Detroit. And the Junior Girls Golf Club was begun in 1989 in Phoenix by teaching professional Sandy LaBauve. That program not only teaches girls how to play, but touches on building friendships and learning to compete. The Junior Girls Golf Club has expanded to another dozen cities.

The LPGA Tour has seen new event sponsors such as Nike, Time Inc., Chrysler and Club Corporation of America get involved with women's golf as a marketing tool.

The Independent Insurance Agent Junior Classic, which for many years included girls within the boys competition, created a girls division in 1993 to recognize the increased interest by girl juniors.

State agencies are taking a stand against golf facilities that discriminate against women, such as one state's alcoholic beverages control commission filing a law that would revoke or suspend the liquor license of any state golf course that wasn't totally or distinctly private if they had exclusionary policies against women. Legislation has been approved in states such as Minnesota, Michigan and California that guarantees women equal access to courses at private clubs. States are making the case that if clubs don't change on their own, they will pass laws that make them.

Women's influence in the area of teaching has increased. They are becoming more accepted as teachers of the swing and able to dispense instruction advice with accuracy and effectiveness. Four universities, Ferris State, Mississippi State, New Mexico State and Penn State, have programs women can enroll in to earn a degree in professional golf management and go into the club professional field. At the end of 1994, Pamela Phipps became the first woman to reach the PGA of America's Master Professional level. In the LPGA, there are around 700 members of its teaching and club professional division.

There is more media coverage of men's golf events than women's. The media blame a lack of interesting stories; women players say the media doesn't look hard enough.

Women players are taking practice and improvement seriously, not just getting a round in once a year and calling themselves golfers. About 29 percent of the golfers who use practice ranges are women.

There has been effectiveness in convincing architects of existing and future courses to look into using a varied set of forward tees, with appropriate landing areas, to reflect the abilities of the beginning, average and better female player. Many layouts are not set up to make it easy for women. These courses were built by men with men in mind as the primary players. So women had one set of tees (usually called the "reds") and men had a variety of two or three tees. Often the women's tee only made the hole a few yards shorter than the regular men's tee. Course architects of the modern era are building courses that reflect the philosophy of multiple tees.

Golf course professionals are seeing how businesswomen are well organized when it comes to golf. Businesswomen have a network of friends and clients. When a club pro helps out a woman, there's the possible reward of the woman bringing an event to the club or new members. Some golf professionals have even gone off site to corporations to give clinics.

Women have flexed their power in the golf shop as prime buyers of merchandise. They demand quality service and products, forcing shop personnel and manufacturers to meet their needs, be creative and innovative. Merchandisers are working to build customer loyalty among women. It's a tough battle since the majority of women still use sporting goods stores and off-course golf shops to buy clubs, balls and bags. They use department stores most often to purchase shirts, sweaters, shorts and slacks. Golf shops have gone to "product grouping" to meet women's needs. This is the display technique of bringing a wide range of products to a central boutique area. Women are also very much involved in decisions for vacation spots and in making real-estate buys, either sharing the decision or being the prime decision maker.

Women working in golf shops have been responsible for increased sales and better service due to their knowledge of the women's market, and in some cases, the men's. PGA club professionals appreciate women shop workers for their creative display ideas, the comfortable atmosphere they create, their sense of style and trends, the women buyers they attract to the shop, and their eye for details and small touches. These women merchandisers know what and how much to buy. Many of them are good players who studied merchandising and worked in fashion retail.

There's much more in store

With all of that action having taken place, women can confidently look ahead to the future with hopes of further advancements. Expect to see additional developments in these areas:

Further refining and improvement of women's equipment, and more understanding on the part of clubfitters to match women with the proper type of clubs.

Continued legislation by states to guarantee that there is equal access for women and other minority groups at private golf clubs.

The attitudes and buying habits of women in the golf shop will not change, meaning golf shop personnel and off-course stores will continue to use friendlier approaches toward women to capture their business. Golf shops will, in fact, continue to employ women in managing positions and have them set up displays and make inventory purchases. Because of this the beginning woman player should receive the proper amount of attention needed to remain interested in golf.

Making golf courses adaptable for different levels of ability will continue. New courses today often have five to seven sets of tees for golfers to select the one that matches their ability level. Primarily the forward tees won't be gender specific. The forward-most tee, for instance, might be best for seniors and women beginners. Gone are the days of saying the shortest tees are for women only.

Junior camps will continue to be effective in attracting not only girls but minorities and the less privileged, who in addition to learning how to swing the club will find out how to *enjoy* the game. Programs will work on making camps less competitive and more social in nature, but still give the better players the edge they need to excel.

Relatedly, instructors will strive to make the game more fun for women, focusing on the individual and giving them a well-rounded look into all the procedures and etiquette involved in playing social golf. Teachers will try to keep women in a comfort zone, helping them feel good about themselves as players.

Expect the national executive women's golf leagues to work with the LPGA Tour in assisting career women to network with the corporations and businesses aligned with the tour as tournament and tour sponsors.

Golf course personnel will refine the idea of family golf, emphasizing programs that serve the entire family.

The talented woman golfer today, already benefitting from better training methods and stronger competitive situations at a young age, will look to sports psychologists and coaches in increasing numbers to get a competitive edge. There is a feeling on the LPGA Tour that to perform well one must be fully committed day after day, so fitness and practice are in and extra socializing is out. This feeling will become more prevalent with women in the college and high school ranks.

The ongoing struggle to get more women to attend women's golf events and appreciate the women's tour more will continue.

Women are increasingly playing more important roles in the work force, thus their roles in making important financial and lifestyle decisions are increasing. How money and time for leisure are allocated within the household will more and more be decided by women, either solely or mutually making decisions. The avid woman golfer spends more on golf than her male counterpart. Women are discerning, though, and want quality service and products. Manufacturers and golf course owners will profit by paying better attention to the women's market.

On the negative side, the LPGA Tour hasn't received the same amount of media attention or television coverage as the PGA Tour. Attitudes will have to change to give the LPGA more publicity when warranted. The media cite poor ratings or sales whenever women are televised or prominently covered as reasons for staying away from them as lead stories. The question will have to be answered: Does the media's lack of coverage accurately reflect the public interest, or would media coverage of women help boost interest in female subjects?

While the future for the female professional continues to improve, the average woman player still battles against restrictions and being misunderstood. At some clubs women can't walk up certain flights of steps, or must walk down a side hallway to avoid passing through the men's grill. There are cramped quarters for women that look minuscule compared to the men's spacious locker space. Expect these antiquated rules and barriers to come down slowly.

Hoping for the best

Why is it so important that efforts continue to improve women's position in golf? Shouldn't they be satisfied with what's happened so far?

Golf's survival doesn't depend on whether women continue to be given equal privileges, just as it doesn't depend on which country wins the next Ryder Cup or Solheim Cup. Golf is beyond all of that because, for those who play it, golf gets into the player's heart and can't be affected by outside forces. But the same people who ask, "Haven't women been given enough concessions?" are the same people who should be asked, "Why is it important that you still have your men's only grill?" If golf is to be for everyone, then everyone must have the same rules off the course as they have the same Rules of Golf on the course.

We can see the effect today of women having better conditions to play golf. The under-25 player, the players coming out of college, are stronger, more fit, more courageous on course, smarter as strategists, and more determined to succeed than any previous generation. Many are proving that you don't have to start playing golf as a toddler to excel. Some start in their mid-teens and earn success through desire and hard work.

The reasons for women playing in the past, however, haven't disappeared. It used to be that women played golf so they could be with the girls in a social setting. Golf was a release from domestic life and fulfilled a competitive instinct. That's not patronizing to say so. Men, it is safe to say, play because being competitive is part of their nature. They want to flex their muscles and be with the boys. Today's woman player has simply brought her competitive edge up a notch and given herself a chance to flex her own golf muscles. Women want to do well, and they can when they set their minds to it.

Playing seriously and being taken seriously. It's what women's golf is all about these days. As a segment of the population affected quite negatively by the game's social problems, women can look to the future with hope that the game's honesty and integrity will win out over discriminatory policies.

GOLFSPEAK: A GLOSSARY OF TERMS

What golf means to: Nancy Lopez, LPGA Hall of Fame member. "Golf is the greatest game of them all. You can play it by yourself and revel in the beauty, solitude, and peace that the game offers. You can play it with your friends and enjoy the camaraderie, good-natured give-and-take, and thrill of competition. You can play it when you're 8 or 80 and you'll learn something new every time out—about golf and maybe about yourself."

How well you intermingle with other golfers not only depends on how good you are at playing the game, but also to what degree you can "talk" the game. You will never feel comfortable on the course unless you clearly understand terms and phrases used as often among golfers as electronic experts toss around computer terms.

Failure to become familiar with golf terminology can lead to some embarrassing circumstances, particularly if you're with an important business associate. For instance, if you are playing a match at your course in the middle of August, your guest might ask, "Are we playing winter rules?" If you don't know that this phrase refers to a break from the Rules of Golf that allows players to move the ball about six inches in their own fairway, no closer to the hole, then you might respond in a way that makes you look like a novice, "Why would you want to play winter rules in the summer?"

Golf has the most wide-ranging collection of words, phrases and terms of any sport. Here is a collection of them to help you "talk the talk" of golf. After reading through this list, you'll understand why many of these words, such as mulligan, parshooter, and hacker, have become part of everyday language.

Ace: Holing out after one shot. See hole-in-one.

Address: Position a golfer takes just before swinging.

Airmail: A ball that carries over the putting green on the fly.

Albatross: Another word for a double eagle.

All square: Tied match between two opposing sides.

Amateur: A golfer who doesn't play for prize money or other compensation.

Angle of approach: Path the clubhead travels into the ball, either downward, level or upward.

Approach: Shot made to the putting green on par-4 and par-5 holes.

Apron: Short-cut grass encircling the putting green. Also called the collar.

Away: The player farthest from the hole; on the fairway and green, this golfer hits first.

Back door: Ball that falls into the hole by entering on the far side.

Back nine: The second nine holes in an 18-hole round; also known as the "in nine."

Backspin: Reverse spin put on the ball at impact that helps it stop quickly on the green.

Backswing: That part of the swing from the start to the top.

Bail-out areas: Course areas where the golfer can safely play toward to avoid trouble.

Ball mark: Depression made when the ball lands on the green.

Banana ball: Ball flight that curves sharply from left to right.

Best ball: Playing format in which the best individual score among teams of two or more players counts toward the final score. Also: better ball.

Birdie: Hole score one stroke less than the par score.

Bite: See backspin; how well the ball stops upon hitting the green.

Blade: (1) Putter with a thin clubhead; (2) Shot hit less than flush; ball is struck by club's leading edge.

Blast: Shot from a bunker when the ball is partially buried.

Blind hole: Hole design in which the fairway or green is hidden from the player's view.

Blind shot: Stroke played to a fairway or green hidden from view.

Bogey: Total on a hole one stroke more than the par score.

Break: Ball movement on the putting green due to the green's curvature and slopes. Golfers must "play" the break to putt the ball in the hole. Also known as borrow.

Bump and run shot: Can be played when the green lacks water or sand in front; player hits a low shot that lands short of and rolls onto the green.

Bunker: Depression in the fairway, rough or near the green. Can be filled with either grass or sand. Golfer must play if her ball lands there. Also called trap.

Buried lie: Ball nearly or completely covered in a sand bunker.

Bye: Exempt from playing a match in a match-play tournament.

Caddie: Person who carries a golfer's bag of clubs during a round and gives advice on club selection and shot strategy.

Carry: The distance a ball travels from its original spot to its point of landing; also, amount of land a ball needs to clear to reach a targeted area.

Cartpath: Gravel or paved road, usually in the rough throughout the course, intended for motorized carts.

Cavity-back irons: Clubs with weight removed from the back of the clubhead and distributed around the clubhead perimeter; best for players who often miss the center of the clubface.

Chili-dip: Usually done by digging a high-lofted club into the turf and moving the ball a few feet; similar to fat shot.

Chip shot: A variety of short shots played around the green, with a low ball-flight trajectory.

Chunk: Poorly hit shot in which the club hits the ground before hitting the ball, severely reducing ball flight.

Close lie: Ball sitting directly on top of the ground with no grass supporting it.

Closed face: Having the clubface aimed left of the intended target line, either at address or during impact.

Closed stance: Standing at address with the left foot closer to the target line than the right (for a right-handed player).

Clubbing: Helping a golfer pick the correct club to play.

Clubface: Grooved portion of the clubhead that makes contact with the ball.

Collar: Short-cut grass area encircling the putting green. See apron.

Course rating: Differs from course to course; the score a 0-handicap player would shoot from a certain set of tees. The more difficult the course, the higher the course rating.

Crosshanded: Unusual grip style used only when putting that puts the left hand lower than the right for a right-handed player, right under the left for a lefty.

Crosswind: Breeze or wind that blows left to right or right to left as the golfer faces the putting green.

Cut shot: A type of pitch shot in which the ball spins clockwise and rises higher and lands softer than normal.

Dew-sweeper: Mis-hit shot that rolls along the ground.

Divot: Piece of grass and turf removed from the ground by the clubhead at impact.

Dogleg: An "L-shaped" hole, usually a par 4, that bends left or right beyond the driving area.

Dormie: Match-play term; a player is dormie when she leads her opponent by the same number of holes left to play.

Double bogey: Hole score two strokes more than the par score.

Double eagle: Hole score three strokes less than the par score.

Down: Side or player losing a match.

Downswing: Swing portion from the top of the swing to impact.

Draw: Hitting the ball so it slightly curves from right to left.

Drive: First shot played off the tee; most often with a driver.

Driving iron: Usually a long iron, such as a 1-iron, used to hit the ball off the tee for accuracy.

Dub: A mis-hit shot; also, term for a poor player who often hits "dubbed shots."

Duck hook: Ball flight that curves sharply from right to left.

Duffer: Nickname for a high-handicap player, similar to dub.

Eagle: Hole score two strokes less than the par score.

Explosion shot: Same as blast shot, hitting a buried ball out of a bunker.

Fade: Hitting the ball so it gradually curves from left to right.

Fairway: The short-cut grass area that is the intended route from tee to putting green.

Fat: Hitting the turf first behind the ball and then the ball; drastically reduces ball distance.

Fellow competitor: In a stroke-play tournament, the relationship between players.

Flagstick: The pole and flag placed in the hole to indicate the hole's location on the green; also referred to as the pin.

Flat stick: Another name for putter.

Flat swing: Golfer's swing that is more horizontal than normal.

Flyer: Ball hit from the rough that has little backspin and thus rolls more than usual on the green.

Flub: Mis-hit shot similar to a fat shot.

Follow-through: Portion of the swing from impact to finish.

Fore!: Exclamation yelled to warn players that they are in danger of being hit by a ball.

Forecaddie: Person positioned in the rough near the driving area to mark where errant drives finish.

Flagstick: The pole stuck in the ground that must be removed while putting.

Forward press: Slight movement of the knee or hands to trigger the start of the backswing.

Forward swing: Portion of the swing from top of the swing to follow-through.

Four ball: Competition in which two golfers play their best ball against the best ball of two other players.

Foursome: (1) Four golfers playing together; (2) Competition in which two-man teams play against each other in an alternate-shot format.

Fried egg: A ball that is half covered in a sand bunker.

Fringe: Closely cut grass immediately surrounding the putting green, same as apron.

Frog hair: See fringe.

Front nine: First nine holes in an 18-hole round; also called the "out nine."

Gimme: A putt of such short length that it is conceded by a golfer's playing partners; violates the Rules of Golf.

Grain: Direction the grass on the putting green lies; affects the break of the ball.

Green: Extremely short-cut grass area used for putting; the hole and flagstick are located there.

Green fee: Price for a round of golf.

Greenies: Betting game awarded on par 3s to the player closest to the hole with her tee shot; usually played that the player must one- or two-putt to win.

Greenkeeper: Superintendent of the grounds crew.

Grip: (1) Putting your hands on the club before swinging; (2) Rubber or leather wrapping on the club used by the golfer to hold it.

Grooves: Scoring lines on the clubface that spin and control the ball.

Gross score: Golfer's score without the use of handicap strokes.

Grounding the club: While at address, touching the ground behind the ball with the clubhead.

Hacker: Nickname for a poor golfer; sometimes just "hack." Can be taken as derogatory, unless, of course, you use it on yourself.

Half/halved: In match play, describes a hole or match that ends in a tie.

Handicap: Number of strokes a golfer receives to equalize competition between poor (high-numbered handicaps) and better (low numbered) players.

Hanging lie: Ball sitting on a severe downslope, and so is above or below the player's feet.

Hardpan: Hard ground without grass.

Hazard: Sand or water areas; you cannot ground your club within them and you usually must take a penalty stroke for hitting into water.

Headwind: Wind blowing into the player.

Heel-and-toe weighting: Club construction method that distributes weight around the perimeter of the clubhead so mis-hit shots are not affected as much.

Heeled shot: Shot hit off the heel of the club; there is a substantial loss in distance.

High handicapper: Usually a beginner; a golfer who receives a high number of handicap strokes, such as 30 or more.

High side: Area above the hole on a putt that slopes right to left or left to right; also called the "pro side."

Hole: Lined, round opening on the putting green that is 4 1/4 inches wide and must be 4 inches deep; also called cup.

Hole high: Ball that stops level with the hole on the green or to the sides.

Hole-in-one: Tee shot that finishes in the hole on a par 3.

Holed out: Ball that falls below the level surface of the hole.

Honor: Playing first on the tee; determined by a coin flip or blind draw on the first tee, by lowest score the rest of the round.

Hood: The toe of the clubface is ahead of the heel, decreasing the loft of the club.

Hook: Ball flight that sharply curves from right to left.

Imbedded lie: Ball that imbeds in wet or muddy turf.

Impact: Exact moment when the clubface and ball meet during the swing.

Inside: Area of ground on the golfer's side of the target line.

Inside out: Swinging the club so it travels inside the intended target line on the backswing and to the right of it after impact.

Intended line: An imaginary line starting from the ball and extending to where the player wants the ball to go.

Intermediate target: Aiming point used to line up a shot to a target.

In the leather: Ball very close to the hole. Original meaning was the length of a leather grip, now thought to be the length of the clubhead to the bottom of the grip.

Iron: Clubs numbered from 1 to 9 and the wedges; the lower the number, the farther the ball travels.

Lie: The longer the club, the flatter the lie angle of the club becomes.

Knee-knocker: A short putt, usually three to five feet.

Knock-down shot: Partial shot hit to cause a low trajectory.

Lag: A lengthy putt, struck so the ball stops within a few feet of the hole.

Lay-up shot: Playing a shot short of trouble, such as a water hazard.

Lie: (1) How well the ball sits on the turf; (2) Current number of strokes played on a hole, as in "What do you lie?"; (3) Angle the back of the clubshaft makes with the sole of the club.

Line of play: Direction the player wants the ball to travel, from where it lies to the hole.

Links: Traditional meaning is a course by the sea; today it is loosely used to specify any golf course.

Lip: Edge of the hole or a bunker.

Lip out: Putt that rims or rolls along the edge of the hole and spins away.

Local rules: Rules of Golf additions that are unique to a golf course.

Loft: Amount in degrees the clubface is angled.

Long irons: Less-lofted clubs; the 1-, 2- and 3-irons.

Low handicapper: Often an experienced player; a golfer who receives a low number of handicap strokes, such as under 10.

Low side: Area below the hole on a putt that slopes right to left or left to right; also called the "amateur side."

Match play: Format in which one person or team competes against another person or team in a nine- or 18-hole match; the side that wins the most holes wins the match.

Medal play: Competition in which the strokes taken for a round determine the standings; professional medal play tournaments consist of three or four rounds; golfer with the lowest score wins. (Also called stroke play.)

Medalist: Lowest individual scorer in a medal play (stroke) tournament.

Middle irons: The 4-, 5- and 6-irons.

Mis-clubbed: Using the wrong club for what the shot required.

Mis-hit: A shot that misses the center of the clubface.

Misread: Playing an improper amount of break on a putt.

Mixed foursome: Competition in which women and men compete simultaneously.

Mulligan: Playing a second ball from the same spot as the first; usually given on the first tee; violates the Rules of Golf.

Nassau: Popular betting game usually played for three points, one each for the front and back nines and one for the entire round, played in match-play style.

Net score: Final score after a golfer's handicap has been applied to the gross score.

Off-center hit: Shot hit on the perimeter of the clubface.

Off line: Shot hit away from the intended target.

Open face: Having the clubface aimed right of the intended target line, either at address or during impact.

Open stance: Standing at address with the right foot closer to the target line than the left (for a right-handed player).

Open tournament: Event that allows both amateurs and professionals to compete.

Out-of-bounds: Area prohibited for play, usually marked with white stakes; hitting shots into these areas results in a penalty.

Outside: Area of ground on the far side of the ball as the player stands at address.

Outside in: Swinging the club so it travels outside the intended target line on the backswing and toward the left of it after impact.

Overclub: Using a club that sends the ball farther than needed.

Overswing: Making too long of a backswing; swinging out of control.

Par: Score a good player would be expected to make on a hole, including two putts (such as a par 4); an 18-hole course usually has a par of 70 to 72.

Par-shooter: Player who makes mostly pars.

Penalty stroke(s): Added to the score as the result of a Rules of Golf violation, such as hitting a ball out-of-bounds.

Pin: See flagstick.

Pin high: See hole high.

Pitch shot: Short shots played to the green with a high-lofted club, giving the ball a high flight trajectory.

Play through: Allowing a faster group to pass a slower group. The slower group should initiate the procedure.

Plugged lie: A ball that remains imbedded within the hole it created upon landing in usually very wet ground.

Posture: Body position during the course of the swing.

Preferred lie: Placing the ball in an improved lie; usually ruled during tournament play when weather has caused muddy conditions.

Preshot routine: Procedure performed in preparation to swing the club.

Press: (1) Hitting beyond a golfer's ability; (2) Betting game in which a losing team may double a bet on the final hole, but does not cancel the original bet.

Professional: Golfer who plays the game for monetary compensation; usually a 0-handicapper or better.

Provisional ball: Playing a second ball when the first is believed out-of-bounds or lost.

Pull: Ball that travels to the left of the target because of a swing flaw.

Punch shot: Lower than normal ball flight; usually played into the wind or under trees.

Push: Shot that travels to the right of the target because of a swing flaw.

Putt: One stroke taken on the putting green.

Putter: Club used to putt on the putting green or from surrounding short-cut grass.

Putting green: Area of very short-cut grass that is where the hole and flagstick are located.

Quadruple bogey: Hole score four strokes more than the par score.

Reading the green: Determining a putt's amount of break. See break.

Recovery shot: An often risky shot made to the fairway or green from a trouble area such as trees or thick rough.

Referee: Official accompanying a group to assist in rulings.

Rim: Ball that rolls over the edge of the hole; same as lip out.

Rough: Tall grass that borders the fairway and surrounds the green.

Round: A complete set of holes, either nine or 18.

Rub of the green: Ball in flight accidentally stopped or deflected by an outside agency, such as a forecaddie.

Run: Ball that rolls a greater distance than normal.

Run-up shot: Playing a shot short of the green and having the ball roll on.

Sandbagging: Playing poorly on purpose to get a higher handicap to use to your advantage in competition.

Scorecard: Card that lists hole pars and local rules and has space for the player to write in her score.

Scratch play: Playing format in which no handicap strokes are used.

Scratch player: A player with great skill; a 0-handicap.

Scuff: A thin shot; also, marking up a ball's cover.

Set up: A golfer's posture, ball position during address.

Shaft: Part of the club that connects the grip and clubhead, usually metal but can be graphite or titanium.

Shank: Shot that flies to the right, caused by the swing flaw of the club hosel hitting the ball.

Short game: Collection of various shots used to play strokes around the green.

Short irons: The 7-, 8-, 9-irons and wedges.

Shot: Swinging the club to hit the ball forward.

Single: One golfer playing alone.

Skins: Betting game in which a set amount of money is won by the player with the lowest score on a hole. If players tie for the lowest score, the money is added to the next hole's total.

Skull: Hitting the top half of the ball because of a swing flaw; ball travels less than normal. Also known as blade or hitting thin.

Sky: Hitting a ball much higher and shorter than normal.

Slice: Ball flight that sharply curves from left to right.

Snake: Making a putt from a great distance that had many breaks.

Snap hook: Ball flight that sharply curves from right to left, much more than a hook.

Sole: (1) Bottom portion of the club; (2) Letting the bottom of the club touch the ground at address.

Square: Positioning the feet, shoulders, knees, elbows parallel to the ball-to-target line.

Square face: A clubface aimed correctly at the intended target either at address or impact.

Staked trees: Newly planted trees that are tagged and held up by a stake; a local rule usually allows players to drop away from staked trees with no penalty.

Stance: Position of the feet prior to swinging the club.

Stiff: A ball closer to the hole than being "in the leather," usually within a couple of inches.

Stony: Ball hit very close to the flagstick; also called hitting the ball stiff.

Stroke: A full swing or putting stroke made with the intent to hit the ball.

Stroke hole: Hole where a player receives a handicap stroke.

Stroke play: Competition in which the strokes taken for a round determine the standings; golfer with the lowest score wins. (Also called medal play.)

Stymie: (1) Situation where shot to the target area is blocked by a tree or other object; (2) An obsolete Rule of Golf; on the putting green, a golfer was stymied if a playing partner's ball was between his ball and the hole.

Summer golf: Playing the ball as it lies throughout the course; playing by the official Rules of Golf.

Sweet spot: The place on the clubface where the ball comes off most solid, usually the center.

Swing: Movement made with a club to advance the ball forward.

Swing length: Distance the golfer swings the club back on the backswing.

Swing plane: Imaginary "plane" the club is swung along from start to finish; connects the shoulders and the ball.

Swing speed: How fast the player swings the club at impact, in miles per hour.

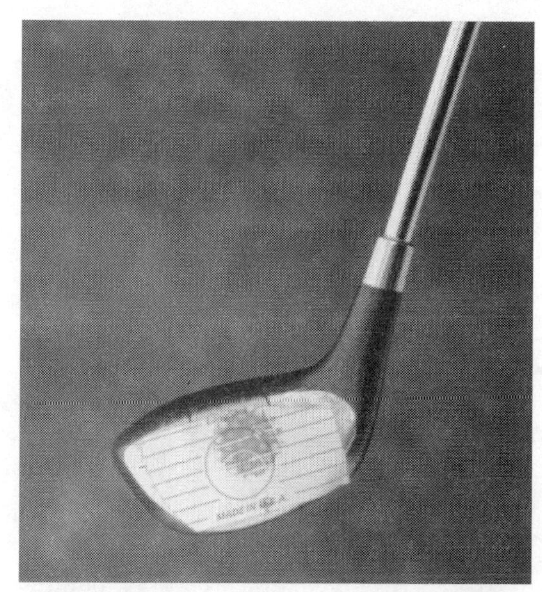

Sweet spot: This impact tape shows that the sweet spot on the clubface is in the center of the club.

Swingweight: Golf club's weight distribution about a fixed fulcrum point. The higher the swingweight, the more the club feels heavy in the head. This is how heavy the club feels when you swing it, not its overall weight. Women should swing a club in the C-4, C-6 range.

Tailwind: Wind blowing from behind the golfer toward the target.

Takeaway: Swing segment from address until the hands reach hip height.

Tap in: Putt of very short length, six inches to a foot in length.

Target: Where the golfer intends the ball to finish.

Target line: Imaginary line from the ball to the target, used to help aim the club and body.

Target side: Side of the body or ball that is closest to the hole or target where the golfer is aimed.

Tee: (1) Wooden or plastic peg used to hold the ball while teeing off; (2) Area of short grass from where a golfer begins play on a hole.

Tee markers: Indicates where golfers should play from on the tee.

Tee off: Playing a shot from the teeing ground.

Tee time: Assigned time for a group to begin play.

Teeing ground: Area of short grass from where play begins on a hole.

Tempo: The speed or pace at which the player swings.

Tending the flag: Holding the flag while it is still in the hole for someone putting from a distant spot, then removing it before the ball reaches the hole.

Texas wedge: Using a putter from off the green.

Thin shot: Striking the top half of the ball; similar to a bladed shot.

Threesome: Group of three players.

Through the green: Entire area of the course except the tee, putting green and all hazards.

Timing: Coordinating the many moving parts of the body to make a functional and effective swing.

Toe: (1) Broad part of the clubface opposite where the shaft and clubhead join; (2) Swing flaw of hitting the ball on the toe.

Top: Swing flaw in which the club comes down directly on top of the ball.

Trajectory: Height and flight pattern of the ball after it's hit.

Trap: See bunker.

Triple bogey: Hole score three strokes more than the par score.

Twosome: Group of two players.

Underclub: Using a club that doesn't hit the ball as far as needed.

Unplayable lie: Ball resting in such a way that the player cannot make a swing; player takes a penalty stroke for moving the ball clear by two club-lengths.

Up: Side or player leading a match.

Up and down: A player missing the green with his approach, but who uses a chip shot and a putt to make a par.

Upright swing: A swing more vertical than normal.

Waggle: Short, back-and-forth movements with the club prior to the takeaway.

Wedge: High-lofted club used for short shots.

Weight shift: Body weight transferred from a centered position to the right side then centered and moved to the left during the swing for a right-handed player.

Whiff: Missing the ball completely while swinging; counts as a stroke.

Wind cheater: A well-hit ball that flies low to avoid being affected by the wind.

Winter rules: Moving the ball six inches from its spot in the fairway, no closer to the hole; violates the Rules of Golf. Similar to preferred lies.

Woods: Wooden- or metal-headed clubs used for shots off the tee and fairway; woods hit the ball the farthest distances of all clubs.

Worm burner: Very low shot that scoots over the top of the grass.

Wrist cock: Hinging the wrists during the swing.

X'd-out ball: Ball with an imperfection sold at a lower cost.

Yips: Muscle nervousness that adversely affects the putting stroke.

BIBLIOGRAPHY

Brown, Gene. *The Complete Book of Golf.* New York: Arno Press, 1980.

Cotton, Henry. *A History of Golf.* Philadelphia-New York: J.B. Lippincott Co, 1975.

Coyne, John. *The New Golf for Women.* New York: Doubleday & Company, 1973.

Dobereiner, Peter. *The Glorious World of Golf.* New York: McGraw-Hill Book Co., 1973.

Lopez, Nancy, with Don Wade. *Nancy Lopez The Complete Golfer.* Chicago-New York: Contemporary, 1987.

Lynch, James and Carole Collins. *Sandra Haynie Golf: A Natural Course for Women.* New York: Atheneum, 1975.

Martin, H.B. *Fifty Years of American Golf.* Argosy-Antiquarian Ltd., 1936 (Reprint 1966).

Suggs, Louise. *Par Golf for Women.* New York: Prentice-Hall, 1953.

Wright, Mickey. *Play Golf the Wright Way.* Garden City, New York: Doubleday & Company, 1962.

Zaharias, Babe Didrikson. *This Life I've Led.* New York: A.S. Barnes & Company, 1955.

Periodicals

Golf Digest

Golf for Women

PGA Magazine

USGA Golf Journal

Women's Golf (a *Golf Digest* supplement)

Associations

National Golf Foundation